"I first came to Dr Michelle after years of doubting myself and my capabilities in my sport. I had had coaches over the years who I allowed to reinforce my negative thinking and while they pushed me to work harder and achieve more, I believed less and less in myself. Without totally knowing it, I created a negative thinking pattern which kept me from feeling good about myself, my goals and my own potential. I was damaged from the past, fearful of the future and stuck in an uncomfortable place.

In our first meeting, Dr Michelle asked me the hard question that I was too afraid to ask myself; she wondered what I thought was so wrong with me that I couldn't achieve greatness? Her approach was gentle and we got right to getting to the root of my insecurities. We went way back to some of my earliest memories and uncovered where my pattern of self-doubt stemmed from. I remember when Dr Michelle first told me that I have a perfectionist mentality and in each performance I would judge myself so harshly if it didn't go as perfectly as I wanted it to. Since my expectations were on things mostly out of my own control, I had no idea how to confront

D1441779

my fears and insecurities; I was a prisoner of my own negative mind.

Dr Michelle gave me so many tools and exercises to begin to retrain my brain. One lesson that has had the strongest impact was about objectivity and not adding anything to my performance or my practice. In the past, I would judge myself based on if something went good or bad, which often left me doubting myself and feeling like I had failed. Instead, Dr Michelle encouraged me to look at the situation with an objective eye. I have learned, and continue to learn, how to live more in the moment of the performance, how to share the performance with my audience, rather than be stuck in my own mind about it. This really helped me to see the bigger picture, to free myself from judgment and open my eyes to a new world of happiness and acceptance. In the end, I was thinking negatively over a past performance, bringing that negativity into each new situation, only reinforcing my own doubts and fears. Dr Michelle helped me to catch the moment this would happen, stop it from happening and to become more present.

next level in my Olympic career I received the help of Dr. Michelle Cleere. My mental barriers were enormous, but Michelle helped me to break down those barriers and overcome the doubts I had about my ability. She gave me the tools necessary to overcome distractions, barriers, and setbacks and helped me excel in sport. Michelle also gave me the tools I needed to capitalize on my strengths making me a better, stronger athlete."

Tracy B., 2X Olympian

"Confidence is one of the most important mental tools that a person can have. Without confidence, it makes it hard to achieve what you want in life. Dr. Michelle Cleere helped me to find my confidence again and overcome the mental challenges that were preventing me from achieving my goals. She gave me to tools to recognize the things that I could and couldn't control in my life. That gave me the confidence to take control of my aspirations and not let anything get in the way.

Dr. Michelle Cleere is to the mind what Muhammad Ali is to boxing. She has perfected ways of helping you overcome your mental challenges."

Lanny B., 3X Olympian

"Before I began work with Dr. Michelle Cleere I was frustrated with the divide between my ability and the results I was getting. Once we got started the results were immediate and pronounced. I began advancing much further in highly competitive, international auditions and having more satisfying performances. She helped me to let go of the details, focus on the big picture and play from the heart. She also helped me to see that my quest for excellence on the stage was directly connected to my pursuit of being a better father, husband, teacher and human. Michelle has been a tireless advocate for my success and I feel very fortunate to have her in my corner whenever I go out on stage or take on a big project."

Professional Orchestral Trumpeter and Instructor of Trumpet

"I met Dr. Michelle when she spoke at a community lecture on bouncing back

from injury. As a runner sidelined by injury, I found her talk encouraging and helpful. She had a down-to-earth style, was very approachable, and obviously knew her stuff. I became an immediate fan and subscribed to her Mental Moments blog. It was one of her posts that resonated with me and prompted me to reach out to her. Although I've always identified myself as being an intense perfectionist and overachiever, I've also harbored feelings of "faking it" and "not being good enough," which I believed affected my ability to advance in my career. When I emailed Dr. Michelle, I was ready to take a chance and make a change.

Dr. Michelle has a process that works. Sessions with Dr. Michelle are productive, actionable, and, many times, enjoyable. Her insights helped me to discover that what had been holding me back were negative beliefs about myself that I had grown up with, and she helped me to replace these with new beliefs about myself that were both positive and better resonated with me-- an endeavor that I was very skeptical about. In time, I had to admit even to myself that with each small success, I began to trust in her process and truly believe in myself and my abilities. In a matter of months, not years, I was feeling SOLID self-confidence, learned better ways to handle emotionally charged situations without getting wrapped up in the emotions, and had a toolbox of proven strategies for tackling other situations that had been triggers for anxiety and self-doubt. Although I went to Dr. Michelle for what I thought was for purely professional reasons, the changes in my perspective and beliefs have benefited all aspects of my life. It's been about a year and a half since I first emailed Dr. Michelle and, while she doesn't think I need to, I continue to see her periodically, just to keep myself "on track.""

L.B.

"Working with Dr. Michelle Cleere to prepare for a Firearms Instructor Bullseye Shoot-off competition was invaluable. Dr. Cleere counseled me on addressing the mental challenges of shooting and guided me to a deeper level of focus that helped to mute the external distractions, internal static and self-doubt. In that focused state of mind, I could truly concentrate on the process of shooting, not the results. Dr. Cleere helped me to see that it is in the process where I have true control and where the actual fun of the competition lies."

Natalie Arnold, Law Enforcement Officer

"Several of my clients have used Dr. Michelle's services when they got "stuck". Mental ruts may be the toughest to overcome and Dr. Michelle has the tools and experience to help guide us through."

Stephanie Atwood, M.A., Founder/CEO
Go WOW Living

"Dr. Michelle is that rare professional who can help you help yourself. She is genuinely dedicated to each and every person she interacts with. Her style is refreshingly real and inspiring!"

L.J.

"Dr Michelle Cleere's techniques and strategies to achieve peak performance are GOLD.

Dr Michelle is the "secret peak performance weapon" for athletes, artists and leaders all over the world and now she has generously made her most powerful work available to all women in her latest book "From Here To There".

I can hardly wait to make Dr Michelle's book a part of the curriculum of all my Business Trainings for women entrepreneurs because there is nothing more important for women in business today as having the mental clarity, the confidence and the focus to powerfully take advantage of every single opportunity"

Ana Rosenberg, Business Success Mentor

My Free Gifts to you

Thank you for buying my book *From Here to There: a simple blueprint for women to achieve peak performance in sports and business*!

Because you've bought my book you are eligible to receive 3 special gifts that no one else has access to:

1. Dr. Michelle's EZINE: "Getting What you Want"
2. The opportunity to apply for a *Confidence to Win* Breakthrough Strategy Session with Dr. Michelle
3. A FREE audio: *Washing the Dishes to Wash the Dishes: An Exercise in Mindfulness*

4. *BONUS gift: get copies of the worksheets from the book*

Get the support and tools you need to get what you want

My research has shown that books all by themselves do not support women in getting what they want in life. That is why I've included 3 special gifts that no one else has access to so that you have the additional support necessary to get what you want.

Your Free Gift URL:
http://drmichellecleere.com/free-gifts/

From here to there

A simple blueprint for women to achieve peak performance in sports and business

Dr. Michelle Cleere

Dr. Michelle Publishing

Printed in the United States of America

Cover Design & Artwork by

Nancy Holliday

Editing by Lydia Puhak

From Here to There: a simple blueprint to help women achieve peak performance in sports and business

Dr. Michelle Cleere

www.DrMichelleCleere.com

Copyright © 2014

Dr. Michelle Publishing

Printed in the United States of America

Cover Design & Artwork by Nancy Holliday

Editing by Lydia Puhak

Dedication

This book is dedicated to my grand-mother, Dorothy Armstrong. She was the only positive influence in my life when I was a child. Her positive and loving attitude is what kept me motivated to live and figure out how to be successful.

This book is also dedicated to my partner, Vivian. She has loved, accepted and supported me as I struggled to find my way in this world.

About the Author

Dr. Michelle Cleere

Dr. Michelle's passion is unlocking the power of the mind so that elite performers can play better and happier. She coaches athletes, musicians, business leaders and other people who need to perform consistently at a high level.

Performance Psychology Ph.D.

Dr. Michelle holds a Ph.D. in Clinical Psychology and a M.A. in Sports Psychology. She serves on the faculty of JFK University. Her research focuses on how the mind can be trained to improve performance and endurance.

Her competitive spirit as a college basketball player and amateur triathlete inspired her to explore sports psychology to improve her own performance. Her big a-ha moment came in 1997 when coaching a team of amateur triathletes, most of whom were beginners. Simple mental skill training, perspective shifts and emotional support yielded almost magical results across the team. People who hated running learned to power up hills with mantras. People who were terrified of swimming in open water overcame their fear with visualizations. Everyone completed their race—including the woman who showed up to the first practice with a snorkel mask and fins—and most kept competing.

Since then, Dr. Michelle has helped hundreds of athletes who compete in sports that require a high degree of mental endurance and toughness such as tennis, golf, triathlon, marathon, cycling, swimming, crossfit, weight lifting, windsurfing, roller derby, rowing, MMA, softball, baseball, biathlon and beach volleyball. She has also worked with concert musicians, songwriters, law enforcement officers, academics competing for tenure and business executives.

Publications

Dr. Michelle collaborates with Dr. Oz, the National Academy of Sports Medicine and Sharecare. She writes about elite performance and the mind-body connection for Golf Teaching Pro Magazine, Triathlete Magazine, USA Triathlon, United States Professional Tennis Association, Professional Tennis Registry. She has authored two books: *Shifting Gears: How Women Triathletes Balance Life with Sport* and *The Experience of Participating in a Triathlon*.

In addition to writing the acclaimed blog, *Mental Moment*, Dr. Michelle has been an expert writer for numerous magazines. She has contributed to articles in *Real Simple*, *Women's Health* and *Men's Health Magazine*.

Collaborations

Dr. Michelle's contributions include: USA Triathlon, Professional Tennis Registry's International Symposium, West Coast Songwriters Conference and Conference on the Value of Play: Collaboration and Creativity in Partnership with IPA/USA, Annual Trumpet Day CSU East Bay and at the US Golf Teachers Cup. She has also been a consultant for Pixar Animation Studios.

For more information visit Dr. Michelle's website: drmichellecleere.com
She can also be reached at drmichelle@drmichellecleere.com

Table of contents

Chapter 1

Chapter 2

Chapter 3

Chapter 4

Chapter 5

Chapter 6

Foreword

Haven't we all said to ourselves "I know what I want I just don't know how to get it?" We may feel like a victim or like opportunity is not available to us when in actuality it is available in abundance if we are willing to look at ourselves, be honest and take on the challenge of changing the way we do things.

I have spent most of my career working to assist people or clients in facilitating outcomes that ultimately rely on behavior change. Whether it be a person trying to lose weight or advance at work to a small business owner trying to figure out why his or her business isn't doing well, it usually comes down to the person repeating behaviors that are not contributing to success. Often these behaviors are subtle but repeated consistently over time they can create a road block on our path to success.

Behaviors are funny things. They originate in our mental and emotional bodies and are not always apparent to us when we look at ourselves. However, it is the mental and emotional behaviors that we choose to employ consciously or subconsciously that can be the cause of our success or our perceived failure. How many times do we find ourselves in a situation with an outcome that seems all too familiar only to wonder why we didn't do things differently this time? We know we should change our approach, our attitude, our level of discipline or something that seems like it would be so simple but then we don't do it. Instead we go down the path of familiarity and employ the same behaviors we have repeated over and over all of our lives.

Most of the time when we don't reach a goal we set, it is not because we didn't want it enough, we weren't smart enough or we weren't talented enough. It is often because we either were unaware of our own behaviors that were detracting from our success or if we were aware, we were not willing to change those behaviors.

So, we know we need to change our behaviors in order to get where we want to go and we want to do it. Now what? Easier said than done, right? It is not always easy to take on behavior change by ourselves. We don't always have the awareness or an unbiased or non-judgmental view of ourselves which is what it takes to begin the process. It can be hard to identify behaviors that need to be changed because they have become so normal to us.

Once we have decided to make the change, we need a plan. We need a path to get from where we are to where we want to go. This too can be difficult to draft on our own because we may be operating from a place of fear of with a lack of confidence in our ability to make the changes needed to get where we want to go.

I have had the pleasure of both working with Dr. Michelle and being the recipient of her wonderful friendship. I have watched Dr. Michelle the professional work with people to realize their true potential, help them be honest with themselves and guide them towards crafting their own destiny. It is truly a skill to be able to ask someone the right questions, questions that open the door to awareness and expose the root of an issue. Dr. Michelle has that skill and knows how to use it in a way that allows a person to discover his or her own truths. Anyone can tell another person what they need to do, but it takes a special talent to be able to guide a person to clarity and to discovering themselves. Once discovered Dr. Michelle makes the bridge between awareness and actualization accessible.

As a friend, I have been fortunate to be on the receiving end of Michelle's unending commitment and support of my well-being and her steadfastness in always checking in on where I'm at along my journey.

We all need a coach, a cheerleader and someone to help us be honest with ourselves. We need that person that helps us hold ourselves accountable and helps us with the tools we need to build our success story. If we look at people who have achieved some kind of success, most did not do it solely on their own. There is usually someone in the background assisting with the process and most often that process is in managing ourselves and challenging ourselves to do things differently and consistently. I challenge you to make the changes you need to make and to be willing to accept help along the way. It will all be worth it.

Laurie Johnson
Vice President, Client Services
Recyclebank

Preface

This is for all the women out there who know they have the potential to be great but struggle to figure out how to get there.

Introduction

I am always saddened by how women see themselves. How you see yourself affects everything in your life: the job you get, the partner you are, the friend you are, the mother you become and the things you do or don't do with your life. The way you see yourself affects your resiliency, confidence, positivity, focus and motivation and in all areas of life. The way you see yourself can impact the way others see you, too.

Unfortunately, most women do not have a realistic view of who they are. 90% of my clients are women. Part of my job with each and every one of them is to open the door to their inner (mental and emotional) and outer (physical) beauty. My wish for you is that you develop the ability to accept yourself for who you really are. You are no better or worse than anyone else. You will never be perfect (no one will) but you are great just the way you are. You were born with the face and body you have. Others enjoy, appreciate and love it, love you and so can you.

As a woman, not only will you tend to struggle to see yourself in a realistic manner which takes away from who you are, but you may very well give to your family and friends in a way that also takes away from who you are. Over the years I've seen an influx of women competing in marathons and triathlons who are in their 40s to their early 60s. What I found is that these women have given up their professions to raise a family and happily so but have lost themselves and are now looking for who they are. It's not conscious but it is the story that I've heard time and time again. Unconsciously women join a marathon or triathlon training group looking not only for a social outlet but also for resiliency, confidence, positivity, focus and motivation.

Women have the strength and the ability to rebuild the skills they need to have to get what they want. It is my commitment and passion to help support women in all of their endeavors by providing them with the necessary skills to get what they want. I've done it with my life and feel that all women can do the same.

Chapter 1: Why you should keep reading

Sometimes when I give a presentation, here is how I begin: "My name is Dr. Michelle. I grew up white trash in a small, rural community in upstate New York. Up until the age of 15 I was obese. I grew up in a household where my mother was emotionally and physically abusive. Around the age of 17 my mother kicked me out of the house for being a lesbian. I packed up some belongings and moved in with a good friend and her family. I quit high school and moved to Louisiana with an alcoholic, abusive lesbian that I had only known for one week. A year later I joined the Army. It was a way to escape everything that had been going on in my life. If you've ever seen basic training in a movie, real-life basic training is exactly how it's portrayed. Six months after joining the Army, I left the Army. I moved back to upstate New York and worked two jobs to make ends meet. Unbeknownst to me I was beginning to develop anorexia. I didn't eat solid foods for eight months. I was hospitalized twice for severe anorexia. The second time I was in the hospital for six months.

I tried committing suicide several times. Before letting me out of the hospital the social worker explained that I needed to have a plan before she was going to let me leave. She suggested college. Although I did get my GED while in Louisiana, being a high school dropout college was never even a consideration. The local community college had an associate's degree in recreation which sounded pretty interesting. The social worker helped me to get an apartment, sign up for food stamps, welfare and register for college. This is shortened version of the 'here' part of my story.

I went on to gain not only an associate's degree, but a bachelor's degree, and a master's degree in recreation. Around the age of 30 I decided to move to California where I started my second master's degree in sport psychology and shortly thereafter my PhD in clinical psychology. I have a partner of almost 11 years and a thriving elite performance coaching practice. This is the shortened version of the 'there' part of my story.

I grew up in a small, rural community in upstate New York. My family was primarily middle-class. My father worked and we didn't see very much of him and for a while my mother was what you'd call a stay-at-home mother. My parents fought all the time and my younger sister always got what she wanted or at least that's how it seemed. So how did I deal with all of it? My first unconscious coping mechanism was food. I remember having an Easy Bake Oven and eating many cakes and lots of cake batter.

I was so fat during most of my childhood years that other kids would make fun of me and some would actually beat on me up. I got picked on all the time. I did not have a lot of friends during this stage in my life.

Not only was I struggling with kids in school but even my own parents made fun of me. They called me Shelly-belly and bouncer. Once when I was in second grade, my mother took me to the doctor and he recommended that she restrict my food intake. She started sending me to school with half a sandwich but I would steal other kids' lunches because I was hungry. How does a fat kid deal with being fat? I dealt with it by eating more food.

I really don't remember much from second or third grade through the end of junior high school. I do remember my parents fighting more and more. Somewhere along the line my mother became abusive to me. I have vivid recollections of her throwing me down the stairs and I remember her slapping me and telling me not to cry or she was going to give me something to cry about.

Around the age of 14 I slimmed down and certain things began to change. I was accepted by some of my peers and started to have friends. I also started to play basketball. Fortunately by the time I hit high school I was a more acceptable teen with friends, acne, and a slimmer figure.

When I was 15 my mother started to have an affair with a married man. My father found out and my parents divorced. It was during this time that my mother's boyfriend's wife came to our house yelling, swearing and making a scene. My father moved out and rented an apartment that was about 10 miles from our house. It didn't actually seem that much different because I never saw him that much anyway.

I remember starting high school as a much different version of myself on the outside but not on the inside. Although I was slimmer and more popular I still had a haunting secret: my parents' divorce and my mother's abuse of me. I became the slave in my mother's house doing the laundry, cooking, cleaning and babysitting my younger sister while most nights my mother went out on the town. When she was home there was never anything I could do to please her as she continued to hit me and scream at me what a horrible person I was.

How did I handle that? I was raised in a very Irish Catholic family. Every Sunday every family member went to church. Initially, being a good Irish Catholic girl I turned to God. Food was my first coping mechanism, God was my second. I never really liked church or God before but figured there must be some sanctity in this religion thing if so many people were showing up each week. I never went to Catholic school but I did attend religious instructions once a week. Now that I think back, did I really need instructions on how to be a good person? I probably did need some instruction and more than most since it was beaten into me that I was a defiant sinner.

The first 15 years of going to church every Sunday did not seem hopeful but again I figured there must be something to it so I started attending

Catholic weekend retreats and at one point was going to church every day carrying my rosary beads with me. I really thought that the church and God were going to help get me out of this jam I was in. At 15, my life was already a mess and I didn't know what to do about it.

At 16 when the church and God didn't help, I started taking diet pills and drinking a lot. My third coping mechanism was taking diet pills and drinking alcohol. There was no freaking way I was going back to being fat. All I had were the few friends that accepted me after I slimmed down, there was no way I could go back to being friendless and alone. In my sophomore year of high school I started drinking before school and after school. By the time I reached my junior year I was definitely not fat but was popping pills daily and drinking like an alcoholic.

During this same time, the one saving grace was sports. My fourth coping mechanism was sports. I did not grow up in a family of athletes or exercisers. As a matter of fact, I did not really do much physical activity until I was 15. Sure I ran around and played freeze tag. I rode my bike a little bit and loved playing football with the neighborhood boys, but it was not until I was 15 that I realized my love for sports.

Entering high school with a new physique surely gave me some confidence so I tried out for cross country. As it turned out, I was a pretty good cross country runner. In the three years I ran I was always in the top 7 and at times in the top 5 of a state championship team. I was pushed hard and in that respect it wasn't so different than growing up in my house but at least I was developing confidence and self-esteem and beginning to feel better about who I was.

I also came to realize that not only was I good at running I was a very good basketball player. I actually had talent. That was the first time in my life I realized I had talent and was accepted for this talent. I was so good at basketball that as a freshman was asked to play varsity.

Although I was good at cross country and basketball and okay in a few other sports I continued drinking and popping pills. I hung out with people who enforced that behavior by accepting me. They may not have been dealing with similar things at home but we were in high school experimenting with sex, sexuality, drugs and alcohol. We were all learning to cope the best way we knew how.

In my junior year of high school my life changed dramatically. I still popped pills and drank a lot but I started dating my assistant basketball coach and hanging out with her friends who were in their early 20's. True story! And what an experience that was for a 17-year-old in a small, rural upstate New York town. Pills and drinking were apparently acceptable but as soon as I started dating my female 20-something assistant basketball coach, wow, all hell broke loose.

Here's how it happened. I was house sitting and decided to have a party. The assistant coach showed up to the party and--voilà--drunken fireworks between the coach and me. Okay, so I don't actually know if there were fireworks because I was so drunk but to this day I just assume there were because we dated for quite some time after that night. Dating the coach included hanging out with her friends, sex and a lot of drinking; which at the time all seemed pretty normal. What probably wasn't so normal was that I was 17 and she was 21 and on days she subbed at

8

the high school, we would find a place to make out during the school day right there on campus.

At some point I realized that the assistant coach was sleeping with several other people and attempting to sleep with several other high school students, even friends of mine. I ended my first lesbian relationship shortly after it began and starting drinking more. I ditched the lesbian but I kept her friends. I had a fake ID and every night of the week I went out with the assistant coach's friends. We had a wicked crazy social calendar. We managed to locate fun places with drink specials every night of the week and if there was a night that didn't meet those criteria we hung out and drank at someone's house. I was drunk every single night and probably most mornings. My junior year was a blur. All I truly remember is having a lot of sex with many women and drinking until I threw up.

I'll bet you are asking where my mother was in all of this. Absent! She was so caught up in her self-centric world that she didn't really pay much attention to what was going on for me. There were those few exceptions when I came home completely drunk and caught her attention, but not in a good way.

After a lot of sex and drinking I finally decided that I must be a lesbian. I was sleeping with women and liked it for the most part at least in comparison to those high school boys I dated for a minute earlier in my high school years. Once I made the decision that I was a lesbian I told my mother and again that caught her attention but not in a good way.

At some point, drinking, sex and being a lesbian at 17 was going to take its toll. There are only so many days at such a young age things can continue moving along abnormally before something breaks. I remember being so hung over in my psychology final that I fell asleep for 95% of my exam waking up with 10 minutes left to complete the entire exam. Needless to say I did not pass that class or probably many others; not that I would remember.

A few short months later, my mother kicked me out of the house for being a "lesbian." I packed my bags and moved in with a friend and her family. It was a pretty good arrangement. I got to hang out with my best friend and her family at least cared enough that I had a roof over my head.

During one of the parties we had I met a lesbian who I really liked. She seemed really cool but was getting ready to move to Louisiana. Having known her for about a week I decided that I would move to Louisiana with her. What did I have to lose? She went to get herself set up and a few weeks later I dropped out of high school and took the Greyhound bus from upstate New York to Louisiana to move in with a woman I barely knew.

There I was, in the middle of Louisiana with a woman I didn't know. Hm! Interesting! Initially things were fun. She had a huge trailer in a trailer park and we lived an okay life. I found a job and spent my money on drinking and smoking dope. This woman was no stranger to drinking. In fact she drank way more than I did and so much sometimes that she would freak out. By freaking out I mean emotionally and physically violent toward me. Alas the reason I even charted these waters. She was exactly like my mother.

I retreated to the sanctity of my job and went to night classes to eventually receive my high school diploma. In retrospect this is one of those events that I am not at all sure how it happened. How does a person in my predicament decide one day that she needs to go and get her high school diploma? Where on earth did that idea come from?

After, oh, I don't know, 6 or 7 months of abuse, I moved back to Upstate New York, alone. I had the unfortunate opportunity to move back into my mother's house. Nothing there had changed except now she had a man living there. I knew it was a mistake but I was 18 and had nowhere else to go so I did what I had to do. I traded my one bad experience for another bad experience. She was still abusive.

Feeling as though I was living in hell (or at least that what the Catholics call it) I walked into an Army recruitment office and joined. I was going to South Carolina and did not have to deal with my mother or ex lesbian lover who were both abusive. It was my grand escape plan.

I showed up in South Carolina very ignorant to the ways of the Army. I had no real idea what I was getting myself into nor had I really even thought about it. From the airport I took a bus with a bunch of girls and boys who looked very much like I did, scared shit-less. We got off the bus and were im-mediately met with shouting, screaming and demands. Yet another experience just like the one I had at home. I sup-pose to a certain degree I felt pretty comfortable with this since I spent much of my life in this kind of environment.

I thought my mother was good at making me feel like crap. The Army was better and quicker at it than she was. In one day I knew who was boss. I had all my hair cut off, I had no choice in what I wore, I had no choice in what I ate, I had no choice in what happened throughout the day, most everyone was yelling at me and I was being told what to do pret-ty much every second.

If you've never been in the Army let me just give you a little tidbit of back-ground. If you've ever seen a movie about people in the Army from what I've seen on TV and experienced in real life they are pretty much the same. Basic training is everything you ever thought and have ever been told. It's pretty much like going to war every day. Take what I wrote above about my first day and multiply that by 6 months. Besides all of that, there was PT, bivouac, the rifle range and mess hall duty. Ah mess hall duty! I felt like I was in a movie one day during mess hall duty. It was my birthday and I had to peel bags and pounds of potatoes by hand for hours and if that wasn't enough I spent the entire evening of my birthday cleaning up the mess hall. I spent the night of my 18th birthday in the Army barracks bathroom crying like a baby while the rest of my platoon was sound asleep.

I finally graduated from basic training (woo-fucking-hoo!) and went to Army school in Georgia. As one might imagine going from South Carolina to Georgia was not a huge cultural shift– two Army bases in two southern towns both with plenty of rednecks and discrimination.

I decided I would go into communications. I suppose because I didn't grow up with any I figured I had nowhere to go but up. During the day I learned how to use the sophisticated Army communication system to communicate to soldiers in the field from my tank (that may be highly classified information) and at night I'd get drunk off my ass. A group of friends used to take me to Cat Man Do (there really is a place called that) and we would drink and drink and all stay together in cheap hotels. It served its purpose at the time which was trying to forget all the Army bullshit.

During this time I ended up being attracted to one pretty little blonde who supposedly wasn't gay. No problem because I had many other suitors on the side: a very nice guy, a married woman, a couple and an older woman who I did end up sleeping with several times. In the Army there were no rules at least for matters of the heart. We were all just trying to find whatever was going to soothe the discomfort of Army life.

About 2 months after getting to Fort Gordon Georgia I began realizing my disdain for Army life. It really wasn't for me and I didn't know what the hell I was doing there. I realized it was a continuation of the abuse my Mom doled out, it was a way for me to get the hell out of Dodge and it was a way for me to get some things figured out, but it was not fun. I started cutting back on eating and realized that my body was depleting. Initially I had gained a little bit of weight in the Army (probably from all the drinking) and figured it must be time to do some dieting. It continued to get worse. I went to my sergeant and told him that I needed to leave the Army because I had some things to do back home. This just so happened to be at a weird time when the Army was seemingly just letting people out, just letting them go home. My sergeant took me to his superior and we chatted. I just told them that I had to leave because I had some things going on at home. They didn't ask too many questions. The next thing you know I was headed home.

Of course later I found out they were going to let me go anyway because they "thought" I was gay. My sergeant came to me and asked me if I was gay. I told him yes and he proceeded to tell me that if I hadn't decided to leave they would have kicked me out anyway. That was well before for don't ask, don't tell was made policy.

I left the Army with more baggage than I went in with. I went back to Upstate New York, found a room (with no view) and started working at Pudgie's Pizza down the street from where I was living (what a paradox, eh?). It all seemed pretty normal but it was hard to live off the money I was making so I took on a second job at Perkins as a waitress. Let's think about that word, *waitress*. I went from being a lesbian, gun shooting (just out of the Army), and heavy drinker to a waitress. I am pretty sure there is a movie in there somewhere. Anyway I was working 2 full-time jobs which I am pretty sure set the stage for my obsessive-compulsive (undiagnosed), type A motivation as I've gotten older.

All the while I was not eating and shrinking away to nothing. I had not eaten solid food for 8 months. I lived off bubble gum and Coca Cola. I am surprised I still have teeth given that and my later routine of throwing up every single day after I ate anything. Finally after 8 months of telling my mother that I had not eaten she decided to do something she had never done and hasn't done since, be motherly. She took me to the doctor who diagnosed me with anorexia. I was 5'9" and probably 120 pounds at the time. Coping mechanism number... oh I don't even know what we're up to now but suffice it to say anorexia was my next coping mechanism.

Life sort of went on. I still wasn't eating but I began going to the therapist in Syracuse. I drove there once a week which probably wasn't a great idea. I had no nutrition and sometimes could barely see because my vision was blurry and my head was so swarmy. One day a few months after I starting seeing the therapist I received a call that I was going to be admitted into the hospital and needed to check myself in the next morning.

So, off I went to Syracuse and was admitted into a hospital psych ward. How interesting it was to be an anorexic admitted to a psych ward. There were some crazy psychotic people on that floor. I was introduced to the nursing staff, they weighed me, I met some of the other patients, and they showed me around the floor. They told me I would be in individual counseling and group counseling every day. I can't remember exactly which meal was my first. I want to say dinner. Regardless that was the hardest, scariest meal I think I'd ever eaten. I had not used a fork or knife for almost an entire year and was forced to use utensils to eat while sitting at this little cafeteria style table with all these other people around. If you imagine what it must have felt like to be one of the first people on earth to use a fork and knife then you can imagine what it felt like for me that very first day.

There I was on the psych ward at the hospital surrounded by crazy people. That sure was the capper for me at that point in my life. What the hell was I doing here? I was just dieting to lose a few pounds and now these people think I am crazy! Sure I wasn't comfortable sitting down to eat a meal using a fork and knife but not everyone uses a fork and knife and they aren't considered crazy.

Needless to say, I didn't eat that first meal after eight months of avoiding food but the nurses made it clear that I would eat and that I would be watched. Watched? Apparently they were concerned that I was going to throw up the food I just ate. At this point I don't remember being a thrower upper (much). I recall throwing up a few times in High school after the basketball team dinner prior to the game. The only reason I did that was because my older friend did it and thought it was cool.

The hospital was a crazy ride. I had to take meds. I got to play a lot of pool during the day. And just like the nurses said on that first day I had group therapy and individual therapy every day and I had to eat three squares. The food situation reminded me of my mother (now you know that can't be good). She would also make me sit at the table until

I ate everything. I quickly learned that if I wanted to get out of the hospital I just had to do whatever they wanted from me to make that happen. I needed to gain weight and they would set me free. So that is what I set out to do. It sounded simple enough.

Christmas came and my weight was up and they let me go home so I could celebrate the holidays with my family. Now who's crazy? This anorexic was headed home to celebrate the holidays with her family. Didn't they hear anything I had said in group or individual counseling about my family??? I was out and off I went. The holidays were fine. It was what came next that wasn't so fine.

When I left the hospital I had the unfortunate circumstance of living with my father and his wife. There was nowhere else for me to go and they lived right outside of Syracuse where I needed to be for therapy. Let me set the stage for you. My father was always so obsessed with his own looks and food issues that there was no way he was going to be able to deal with mine. He was also obsessed with how much his wife ate and spent much of his time making fun of her for being fat. Even as sick as I still was I wanted to slap the shit out of him every time he talked to her like she was dumb. My father's wife was wayyyyyy too nice. She took everything he doled out to her. My father would make it seem like he was cajoling her sometimes so that she'd laugh but everyone knew he was just hiding the fact that he was being rude, insensitive and mean to her.

So there I was in the midst of my father's crazy relationship with himself and his wife. Their job was basically to make sure I ate and didn't throw up. They were my new watch-me-eat nurses. I ate but they didn't do such a good job making sure I didn't throw up. Every night I would go out for a walk immediately after dinner so I could throw up and they never caught on.

After a couple of weeks my father decided that I needed to look for a job. He did not want me sitting around all day. I started looking for a job but actually spent most of the day obsessed with my weight, throwing up, laxatives and exercise. I never ate much but did start accruing an appetite. Since I didn't want to keep that food inside of me I started throwing up two, three, five, or even 10 times a day.

There came a point in time when I started being recruited by colleges to play basketball for them. I was good in high school, but had dropped out. I couldn't imagine that two colleges now wanted ME to play basketball for them. But they did. In the midst of darkness came light but it didn't last long. I was asked to go to a basketball game where the two teams that were recruiting me where playing each other. It was exciting. I got to sit behind the bench and watched the entire game up close. After the game both coaches came and talked to me for a while and I had to choose which college I was interested in. I decided I wanted to go to Keuka College (an all-girls school at the time). Keuka College was just up the road from where my grandmother lived. I spent a lot of time as a young kid roaming around the college grounds. It was on a lake and the campus was gorgeous. I set up a meeting with the coach and explained to him that I was really excited about getting a scholarship. The coach said he was really glad that I had chosen Keuka College but that he sadly had to retract his offer because he said I was too sick to play. That was one of me most painful experiences of my life. I had spent hours practicing basketball on the playground and in the gym in hopes of playing in college. I seemed like my big chance had come and gone in a matter of moments. My hopes and dreams were smashed in an instant.

Good news was, I found a job. Yep! I was going to work at Friendly's ice cream shop as a short order breakfast cook. It actually sounded like fun. I had always wanted to be a chef but my therapist told me that wasn't a good idea because I was an anorexic. She said it wasn't good for me to be working around food. It was a good time to give that theory a try.

I really did like my job at Friendly's but my therapist was right; it probably wasn't the best environment for an anorexic. I looked at and smelled food all day but never ate it. I went into work at 4:00am because I had to prep for breakfast and be ready when the doors opened at 5am. When 5am hit it was crazy busy. I had to hustle to make French toast, fried eggs, poached eggs, bacon, sausage, and pancakes all at the same time and for several people at once, but I liked it because it took my mind off of everything else. I even got to scoop ice cream and make shakes and sundaes. I really loved that.

All the while loving my job I was not eating and going home to be under the *watchful* eye of the parents. Once again I was losing weight but no one seemed to notice and no one seemed to care except for my therapist. 3-4 months after I left the hospital I found myself right back in there and in a worse state than the first time.

Not only had I lost a lot of weight but I was in a dark place with no hope in sight. I was down to around 118 lbs. when I went into the hospital and this time I didn't want to get better, I didn't want to get out and I didn't want to live. I wouldn't eat. I wouldn't take my pills. I walked the hallways with a blanket over my head. I didn't do any of the things I knew I should do. I couldn't. Why bother. Who cares?

Family therapy started and it was awful. My mother blamed me, my father didn't know what the hell to say and I was getting sicker. I continued to lose weight. I got down to 110 lbs. At 110 lbs., I began to feel suicidal. I left the hospital on a pass and bought a package of diet pills, came back and took every single one of the 24-pack. The doctors pumped my stomach. I had to drink charcoal. But hey, it got me some attention and not the awful attention that came from my mother and father, this was nurturing and loving.

I ended up on "watch" and in padded rooms for quite a while because now I truly was crazy and suicidal and wouldn't eat and was skinny as hell. I thought I was a lost cause. I was going to individual and group therapy regularly and was getting pretty good at pool because that was all there was to do. Months passed and I finally got another day pass. Once again I went out on a day pass and did damage to myself. I burned a hole in my arm using cigarettes and matches. You can imagine what ensued. I was just not getting it nor was I doing well.

I can't really remember the day things started to turn around for me but they did and I started following the program again. I began eating, putting weight on. I had been in the hospital for about 6 months and one day the social worker met with me. She told me that the only way I was getting out of hospital this time was if I had a plan. We talked about that plan. Part of that plan was getting on welfare, getting food stamps and then she mentioned going to college. The college part began to give me hope and I began going through local college catalogues to see what might interest me. I had never thought seriously about going to college but this was my chance.

This was the first moment of real clarity in my pitiful little life. I knew that this hospital social worker was not going to let me leave the hospital until I had a sense of what I wanted to do with my life. She was actually the first person who seemed to make any sense in my fuzzy little brain. I'll bet right now you are wondering how something so seemingly simple made such a huge impact. I don't know. I went all this time unable to get beyond my crappy circumstances and some stranger comes along and mentions college and my life begins to change.

Shortly after that conversation I enrolled in college. I was living in my own apartment and stocking my own refrigerator. I was still unsure about eating but going to college and having my own apartment was fantastic. For the first time ever in my life I knew what it felt like to be a fairly healthy, productive adult.

That initial college experience was great. I got an AA in Recreation from a community college and was a dean's list student. I played some college basketball, made some friends, met some girls and lived a fairly normal life. I cooked food, I was social and I went to school.

As I was finishing my associates degree I decided to get a bachelor's degree in Recreation from SUNY Cortland and went on to get a master's degree. My weight and diet was still erratic but better. While pursuing my master's degree another interesting challenge presented itself. I was diagnosed with severe disabilities. As I graduated with my bachelor's degree I continued to be a dean's list student but during my master's degree my grades began to drop. For the life of me I couldn't figure out what happened. A colleague said she had noticed a few things and asked me if I had ever been tested for learning disabilities. I said no. Got tested and sure enough it was discovered that I had severe difficulties with reading comprehension, writing disorder, dyslexia, and seasonal affective disorder. Ugh! Now what? Another obstacle!

Professors told me I would never be able to do it but I worked hard despite their opinions. I developed confidence through the support system I found at the disability center. I worked with the State to get a word processor and my text books on tape. It was not easy but I did it--I figured out how to make it happen. I was one of the only people to pass my entire comprehensive exam on the first try. ☺

Nothing will stop me now. I continued to fight anything that got in the way of my success. I took on adversity as a challenge to make me stronger. Right after I graduated with my MA I had a conversation with my partner at the time about heading to Clemson University to work in an internship there. Clemson was partnering with rural southern communities to set up formal recreation systems in those communities. Off I went to a rural community in South Carolina.

Boy was I in for a surprise. South Carolina was hot, buggy and the people talked funny! I think I was the only white Yankee lesbian in this rural South Carolina community. There were more churches than people there and they had a "white only" pool. My job was to set up a formal recreation system and that is what I did.

Meanwhile my partner had an affair and told me over the phone that she was dumping me. Yay! I left South Carolina for a while to go back to Syracuse to talk to my partner about what was happening and came back a bit broken. I stayed in South Carolina for the entire summer and did manage to find some diversions but once I finished my internship went back to an empty lonely house and no girlfriend.

Throughout all this, I hadn't been doing much running and I kinda missed it. I started running again and not running to lose weight but running to eat. I began running with Frontrunners, a gay running group and met a lot of really nice guys who soon became my besties. I was feeling pretty okay. I still cooked food, I was social, I went to school and now I added healthy exercise to the mix.

A few years later I decided that I wanted to move to CA. Moving out of upstate NY was one of the best things I could have done. Life wasn't simple and easy by any means but it was important for me to get out of the environment I'd lived in most of my life and to do some-

thing different that hopefully would continue to improve my life.

I started doing research to figure
out how to make a successful move to
California. In my research I came across
information on becoming a VISTA volunteer. As I looked more closely I came to
learn that several universities across the
country were hiring VISTA volunteers to
do community service work. Some were
in California and that is when my decision became clear. I applied to the
VISTA program and quickly began getting phone calls from sites who were hiring. Some were prisons, some were
community organizations, and several
were colleges and universities. I was
getting excited.

One of the phone calls I received
was from Fresno State University. The
director of a community service program
was really interested in having me come
there to work. He was very nice and
very supportive. He spent a lot of time
explaining this program and was very
thorough in explaining what my job
would be. Based on that conversation, I
made my choice to go to Fresno State
and work with students in their community service program.

I had one week before I needed to be there. My best friend Kathy and I packed up my Honda with whatever would fit and we drove across country. We stayed in various cities along the way. We ate at funky restaurants. I got pulled over twice for speeding; by the same cop. My friend Kathy learned how to drive a stick shift. It was hilarious. We had fun on our cross-country trip.

Our last night before Kathy was to fly back to New York we stayed in LA. We soon found out the hotel we had chosen was in one of the worst parts of LA. Neither one of us got any sleep. The next day I drove Kathy to the airport, we said a sad goodbye, and I made my way to Fresno.

Fresno started off pretty well. My VISTA volunteer supervisor and his wife generously accepted me into their home until I was able to find a place of my own. Even though I made barely enough money to get by, the work at Fresno State was new and exciting. I really liked it. Everyone was very supportive. The community helped find me an affordable apartment and also helped me to furnish it.

I started getting into swimming. My VISTA volunteer supervisor who was a swim instructor at the local pool invited me to swim with his group. I started to meet people and make friends. I met several guys who I started to swim, run, and bike with. This was my first entrée into the triathlon scene.

After completing my year as a VISTA volunteer, I took a job teaching outdoor recreation at Fresno State. I decided that I liked teaching college students. I lived in San Diego for a short period of time after that. After one year in Fresno and six months in San Diego I finally made my way to Oakland, California. When I first came to Oakland I took jobs working for Peet's Coffee and doing childcare at the YMCA. I soon realized that my master's degree in management of leisure services was not really what I wanted to be doing. One day I came across the sports psychology program at John F. Kennedy University. I could totally imagine myself doing something that included sports and psychology. I was completely intrigued by the idea. So the next thing you know I was registering to start another master's degree, this time an MS in sport psychology. I went through the sport psychology program and loved it. I knew I had found my passion.

Immediately after I finished my degree I decided to get my PhD in clinical psychology and start working with clients. I was involved in a relationship with a woman who lived in Los Angeles which meant we had a long distance relationship. After a year I decided to move to LA. I worked at the Hollywood YMCA and continued to finish up my PhD in clinical psychology. Life was difficult in terms of trying to figure out exactly how I was going to make it and how I was going to keep it all together, but I did it. I started training heavily for triathlons and became sponsored. I spent my days working, studying and training. I made some friends while I was in LA but meeting people was difficult.

One day I decided to reach out to the LA triathlon club to see if I could find some people to work out with. They had a gay discussion board so I posted my plea to find someone to work out with. I got one response from a Vivian Grimaldo. We started training together, having dinner together and became good friends.

A year into my LA experience everything was going well except my relationship. I ended my relationship, moved into an apartment and continued spending my days working, studying and training. During this time Vivian was also in the process of breaking up with her girlfriend and we started to realize that our friendship was developing into something more. Well, it ended up turning into something way more. 11 years ago we moved from LA to Oakland, bought a house, completed our first ironman and set course to set up our professional careers.

Now it's 2014 and after all this I can honestly say that I am a completely different person. Vivian and I still live in our house in Oakland with our three cats and dog. She has a thriving hair coloring business and I have a thriving elite performance coaching practice. I feel as whole and happy as a person probably could be on an individual basis and as part of a couple. This doesn't mean that things are perfect but things are good. Things are much better than they were 40 years ago.

Why am I telling this story? I can also honestly say that without all of what's happened in my life I would not be where I am today. Sure it was a hard road and sure it took longer than probably necessary but it was worth it. If I can take this 50 year journey and get to where I want, I believe you can to. ***From Here to There*** is me laying the landscape to help you take the journey. It doesn't have to take 50 years and the change doesn't have to be this dramatic. What's important is that you do it. Figure it out. Don't let your life *just be* because it's what you've been doing. Take the chance to figure out what you want and go for it. We have unlimited potential and peak performance is not out of your reach.

I've learned how to cope and deal with obstacles differently. Part of that came from my life experiences, part through my education and part through the work I do. Life is not always easy but you can learn to deal with what's not easy while also accepting what is easy. Life is about being able to hold both places in your hands.

- I had to develop my awareness of what wasn't working and where I wanted to go and develop a plan for bridging the gap. I am going to help you develop awareness for bridging your gap.
- I had to learn to build resiliency, increase confidence, not be negative, find motivation and be fo-

cused. I am going to give you information to help strengthen 1 or more of these areas.

- I had to see my vision to know if it was the right path. I am going to help you clarify and develop your vision.
- I had to develop goals and learn to structure life in a realistic way. I am going to help you start to build the landscape.
- I continue to grow and understand this is the process of life. I am going to help you understand this process, too.

The landscape laid out in the pages of this book is going to help you understand how to think about and achieve peak performance in whatever you do. It's not as difficult as you might think. That's not to say that it's not hard but if you're patient, present and willing to chip away at it, you can do it. It's also going to help you think about how to work smarter.

After you've made the decision to make change the proceeding chapters will give you a template for how to think about change and how to move through it. It is the formula that I use with each and every one of my clients.

Chapter 2: Ugh emotions

Intro

My story is a painful example of long periods of working hard despite circumstances and setbacks. It wasn't until years later when I had a chance to take a nice, long look at myself that I began to see that I was learning not to work hard but to work smart. Although I didn't know it then, it was while undergoing those moments of sustainable change—that change that endured and lasted despite my circumstances and setbacks—that I was somehow developing a system from those experiences that became who I was; who I am. I became honest with myself. I chose to change the way I met the challenges in my life by working smarter. I began to see that change is not about working harder and longer but it's about working smarter. What do I mean by this? Have you ever done something that you felt like you put a lot of time and energy into and still didn't get the results that you wanted? It's a common occurrence. In these situations we work physically harder. We ask ourselves, what can I do (physically) to improve this situation? This is immediately where our brain wants to go. When I say that the key is working smarter, what I mean is developing a mental plan that enhances your physical plan so that you don't have to work longer or harder to get the results you desire—working smarter.

Acknowledging emotions

I want to start by acknowledging that we have emotions and define them. Emotions are a funny thing. They can be positive, for example, happiness. They can be negative, for example, fear. Positive or negative can be exactly that and nothing more but many times we put too much stock and energy into them and make them something they are not. Emotions are like a bonfire. The more wood you put on the fire the higher and out-of-control it gets. Emotions are similar. The more fuel you add to the emotion the bigger it becomes.

Positive emotions

People don't regularly recognize positive emotions. Even though positive emotions feel so much better than negative ones they don't always make up the bulk of a person's life experience. In times when it feels as if there are far fewer positive emotions, they feel much more temporary and elusive and we learn to disregard them. This (and several other factors) leaves people focused on negative emotions which give the perception that negative emotions far outweigh positive ones.

There is also a misperception about positive emotion. For example, you are either happy or you aren't. People are in search of a happy life but disregard happy moments. In reality, we can't be happy 100% of the time. What we can do is redefine *happiness* or a *happy life* by paying full attention and creating happy moments.

Negative emotions

Negative emotions rule people's lives. People get stuck on and in them. They start to define us. They rule our existence. There is negativity all around us. I believe that every situation has a negative element to it but it also has positive. We've learned that if we aren't happy then we are unhappy.

Why negative emotions hang on so long

Negative emotions tend to last longer because we spend more time and energy on them. When a negative emotion creeps in we think "what is wrong with me" and start to ruminate on it until we (almost) can't think about anything else. We get trapped in a web of fear, guilt, and anxiety.

Don't allow emotions to be an adversary

- Acknowledge the positive things that happen.
- Redefine positive. It's not just all or nothing; black or white.
- Learn to not ruminate on negative emotions.
- Learn to think more positively.
- Understand that life encompasses positive and negative.

Separate yourself from what you do

We experience emotion, period. I understand that what you do is a part of you and you are a part of what you do but it's important to separate yourself from what you do. It's not personal and it's not who you are. Let me explain.

Many people take what they do and use it as a personal attack of who they are. For example, when I don't perform the way I think I should, as an athlete or at work, I assess that I am not a good person. Is that really true? This is emotional and you are making it personal.

What you do should not be so attached to your person. The only way to be great at what you do is to let go of the emotions, stop any personal attack and start getting objective about what you are doing. One way to start doing this is to take the 'I' out of your statements. Another is to learn to only evaluate the work and not you as part of the work.

Recap

We have emotions but most of the time we don't acknowledge their presence. If we do acknowledge them we pay far too much attention to the negative emotions allowing them to almost rule our existence. It's not only important to acknowledge that we have positive AND negative emotions but to put them into perspective. For example, in any given situation making a global statement that the entire situation was horrible may not be accurate. Try to start looking at situations in a more realistic sense. For example, one of my performers would frequently say that her entire performance was terrible. After we drilled down she started to realize that there were moments that needed improvement but that the rest of the performance was good. In addition, we worked on separating her as the performer and her as the person. Both of these things made a huge difference.

Stop

After a situation when your self-critical voice would normally kick in, reflect on it instead. Leave *I* statements out and only evaluate performance. I suggest you do this using the sandwich approach.

- Start with a positive statement. What went well?
- What didn't go as well? By writing it down you are calling it out, getting it out.

- What one positive or fun thing that happened? You want to end writing a reflection feeling good otherwise the negative has an opportunity to spiral out of control.

You'll notice there are no I's in these questions. This process helps you to become more objective and allows you to see the positives. The last step could be to write these on three sticky notes or note pages in your phone and delete the negative reflection. Why? It's ceremonial of letting go and your brain is always going to remember what didn't go as well as you would have liked it to. Always!!

Chapter 3: Envision it-try it on and see how it feels

Intro

I truly believe that in order for you to get what you want you need to be able to see yourself there, doing it. If you are able to define what your future looks like you will then have the ability to work towards that. You also allow the universe to bring energy geared toward helping you get what you want. You'd be amazed at how getting clear on what you want and setting clear intentions opens you up for those things to happen.

Often my clients talk about wanting to be a great athlete, musician, artist or business professional. They know they want to be great but what they don't often know is what great means. It's important to realistically, define great. Once you define it, try it on. For example, for a while I thought I wanted to be a full-time college professor. I started envisioning myself as a full-time college professor and realized that it didn't feel right.

Envision it

Envisioning the thing that you want gives you a sense of whether or not you really want it. Is that really what you want? When you see yourself there or getting it, how does it feel? What is your intuition telling you? What is your gut saying? It's not until you get clear on what you want and what you expect that you are able to work toward it and get it! If it doesn't intuitively feel right, my suggestion is that it's not right. Move on. If you've envisioned it and it feels good the next step is to see yourself getting it. To do that I recommend you use imagery.

From envisioning it to actually getting it

Imagery is a form a stimulation that is similar to real sensory experiences except the experiences happen in the mind. Through imagery you can recreate previous positive experiences. Recreating past positive experiences involves recalling from memory pieces of information stored from your experiences and using them to shape further meaningful experiences. Your mind remembers these events and recreates pictures and feelings of them for you to use for future events. Through imagery you can also create events that have not yet occurred. For example, a beginning golfer who has not yet had many real experiences with the sport can begin creating initial positive experiences of their own by observing others. A beginning golfer can begin to view other golfers practicing and competing and begin to create positive experiences that will help shape future behaviors. If you have ever watched a great golfer mentally rehearse those moments or you've watched someone you thought was a great putter and tried to mimic that person's putting or you've watched a professional golfer on television and tried to copy their putt, all of this is your minds way of remembering events and creating pictures and feelings of them.

Imagery should include as many senses as possible. Think of your favorite movie. If you were watching the movie but had no sound, what would your experience be like? What if you had sound but no picture? Now imagine you were watching and listening to your favorite movie and you could taste, smell and feel everything going on in that movie. How would that change your experience? Lastly, you have probably attached a variety of emotional states to your favorite movie: sadness, laughter, anger, and so on. Because we use so many of our senses when we watch a movie, it feels like real life and that is why we watch it. Imagery works much the same way.

You can generate information from memory that is essentially the same as an actual experience. Because you can do this, those images can have an effect on your nervous system similar to the original or actual experience.

Psychoneuromuscular theory: when you practice using imagery, you imagine movements without actually doing them. Small impulses fire from your brain to your muscles with the exactness that you are imagining as if you were physically acting.

Cognitive theory: the blueprint (map) in your mind is changed through imagery. For example, if you've run for years with your arms swinging across your body you will automatically do that out of habit every time you run. However, if you learn that a better arm swing positioning is straight back and forth, you can help change your mind's blue-print by using imagery.

Put it together

Think back to a time when you were in your zone. Now recreate that experience by writing down as much as you can remember. Start by writing down bullet points and then build a story using them. Write as if you were going to explain to someone what it felt like, what you were aiming for, and what that would look like. After you've written the story go back through and take out any negative words. Go back through again and add any sensory information: sight, sound, taste, smell, or touch.

If you can't remember having your own past positive experience, the next best thing is to use someone else's. Most of us know someone we think of as a role model that we look up to. Think about what makes that person a role model. If you have a DVD of this person, watch it and think about what makes this person a role model.

When to use

- Use snippets during your day whenever you have a moment, particularly in times when you are thinking about it, more particularly when you are having anxiety or thinking negatively.
- Incorporate imagery into your dreams. Think about your imagery piece prior to going to sleep. This will help it to remain fresh in your mind and allow your sub consciousness to carry it over into your dream state.
- Use imagery as part of a routine. A routine is a way of positively structuring your experience to keep you focused on the task at hand.

Imagery takes practice

Everything we do in life takes development, support, and refinement. None of what we do is (really) automatic. Imagery takes practice. You need to develop your piece of imagery. You need to support it by giving it the time it deserves through patience and practice. You will want to work on refining your piece of imagery by providing more vividness (using more senses) and better controllability (learning to manipulate your images so they do what you want them to).

The benefits of imagery

- Imagery can improve concentration. If you are focused on what you want to do and how you want to do it, then you won't be focused on unrelated elements that detract from your goal or distract you.
- Imagery can build confidence. Visualize yourself taking control and being successful.
- Imagery can help control emotional responses. If you are feeling lethargic imagery can get you pumped up. On the other hand if you are feeling uptight or anxious imagery can help reduce those symptoms.
- Imagery can help you acquire skills. You can practice skills to fine tune them or realize weaknesses and then visualize correcting them. Research clearly concludes that combined with

physical practice imagery can produce superior skill learning.

- Imagery can help you cope with pain or injury. Imagining the healing of an injured area can speed recovery. Using imagery to practice drills help keep skills from deteriorating during injury.
- Imagery can help solve problems. When you are not performing at expected levels of performance, imagery can help you imagine current performance and compare that to more successful performances to find out where the problem is.

Recap

As children we reveal considerable imagery capabilities but are quickly taught to neglect this form of thinking to develop our analytical and language centers. Fortunately, although we are taught not to, we can still utilize that area of our brain. Much like a muscle is strengthened, imagery skills can be regained through practice. It's not magic. It's a human capacity that few athletes have developed to its potential and most people have chosen not to use.

Stop

Ask yourself the following questions:

- Is that really what you want?
- When you see yourself there or getting it, how does it feel?
- What is your intuition telling you?
- What is your gut saying?
- What positive experience did you already have doing this?
- What does your role model look like doing this?

Chapter 4: How change happens

"By any objective measure, my athletic career was wildly successful, but I wish I could time travel and do it all over again with Michelle on my team. The adversity I faced would have been less painful and the wins would have been sweeter. Thankfully, retirement and 'real life' last longer than my sport career, so I have plenty of opportunity to use the mental tools she's given me. It's stunning to see what happens when you shine light on your strengths, passions and personal power and I wouldn't have truly figured that out without Michelle's brilliant questions or personal example."

Professional & Olympic Athlete/Speaker/Author.

Intro

Change does not happen in a second, minute, hour, day, week or necessarily in a month. Change takes time. In my work with clients this is one of the most important yet hardest points to get across to. We live in an information society. We also live in a society that largely accommodates instant gratification. We get on the Internet looking for a pair of sneakers, type it into the search bar and immediately several manufacturers and websites pop up. You find the website you want, you click on it and off you go. As soon as you get to the website, you find the size and color you want, put in a credit card and shipping address and find it at your doorstep in a matter of days. This is the society that we live in. Unfortunately change doesn't happen quite this fast.

Much of the literature says that change takes approximately six months and from what I've seen in my work with women that is just about right. It takes about six months to be aware of what it is that's getting in your way, developing some strategies for peak performance and reinforcing the new strategies so they replace the old ones.

Thinking that you want to make change can start quite quickly. Even starting to think about how to make change can happen quite quickly. It's all dependent on you. If someone is really motivated to move forward in making change the process can start happening on day one with awareness. Awareness is the start of the chains of events known as behavior change.

How our childhood experiences shape us

As we are growing up we unconsciously pick up things in our environment and figure out how to deal with those things. For example, if mom and dad are having a fight, as kids we figure out how to deal with that. How we deal with things as a kid is not always the best, but at the time we are doing the best we can to cope with the situation. We unconsciously find ways in our environment to soothe ourselves so that we can feel better about whatever is happening in our environment that feels uncomfortable. For a child, when mom and dad are fighting it is probably a very uncomfortable situation. How does a young child deal with that? Some kids might cry, wet the bed, lock themselves in a room, suck their thumbs or eat. Let's use eating as our example. Here again is a common coping mechanism for kids. Why? Food is readily available and it is soothing. Mom and dad fight and you grab for the 1 pound bag of M&Ms to soothe yourself. Here's another example, dad has had a rough day at work and comes home with junk food.

For the child, dad is sending a message that after a rough day it's okay to eat junk food.

As you get a little bit older that coping mechanism sticks with you. You have a fight with your partner or friend and you grab for a bag of M&Ms. You have a rough day at work and you bring home junk food. The process happens so unconsciously that you don't even know it's happening to you. Before you know it you get to a point in your life where this has been the way that you've coped for years and years and you don't know anything differently. It's not your fault. When you were a kid you had to figure out how to cope with situations that were happening around you and you did to the best of your ability. But as you got older you were able to recognize that the same coping mechanisms didn't work for you.

As we get older some of us realize that what we're doing isn't working. That generally happens because of education and life experience. With that realization, some people are able to figure out how to make change while others remain stuck in their old coping mechanism. Why? When you've been doing the same thing over and over

again for 20, 30, 40, 50 years it becomes a part of who you are; it's how
you react and respond. A situation happens in your life and without thinking
you react or respond. For many that reaction and response is based on what
you learned as a child. It's been reinforced for 20, 30, 40, and 50 years and
it becomes safe, comfortable and familiar and is our automated reaction and
response to situations. Because they
become automated, they feel like they
are out of our control but they are not.

Something just isn't working any-
more

As you move through childhood
into high school and college you start to
realize that something is not quite right.
The demands and pressures of school
and sports increase and bring with them
an increase in anxiety, worries, doubts,
fears. Although something doesn't feel
quite right you are not able to figure out
what it is. You know something is getting in the way but are not sure what it is
or what to do with it.

As adults, some women continue
to be very aware that something is not
working for them but they are still not

quite sure how to change it. They keep moving along the path they are on feeling unhappy, dissatisfied and out of control. They are busy raising a family and working, which takes their attention away from trying to figure out how to take care of themselves. They are, thus, unable to deal with whatever is not working.

For others, something in life becomes increasingly important in the areas of performance or business and you are immediately confronted with a flood of uncertainty. You start worrying about what people think about you, how you're going to do the perfect job and whether or not you can even do the job. Something that you've taken on really matters to you and it changes the amount of pressure that it puts on you. This is not to say that things didn't matter before but for some reason what you're doing now is of greater importance to you.

Change comes in stages

Because you are so used to thinking in certain, automated ways, changing those thought patterns...phew can be difficult! The way you react and respond has become so ingrained and so involuntary that it feels like it's out of your control. The challenge is that it's not out of your control. When I talk to women about this I initially see a look of relief following by panic and fear. Initially they are relieved that change is possible and that they are in control but therein also lies the problem, I am in control of it but how do I change it. 😃 That combination tends to leave them feeling a little overwhelmed.

All change takes time and patience. You cannot go from being completely negative to completely positive in a day. You will not be able to go from lacking confidence to being completely confident in a week. There is no way to go from being unfocused to being completely focused in a month. This is important to know because somewhere in our brains we think, "OK, I have control over not beating myself up, I know what to do to change it and voilà! it's gonna happen today!"

In behavior change there are stages. In each of the stages, a person has to grapple with a different set of issues and tasks that are relate to making change. Figuring out where you are in the change process is about honesty. You have to ask yourself the hard questions. Are you ready to do what it takes to get what you want? The stages are as follows:

1. Not yet able to acknowledge that there is a problem that needs to be changed.
2. Acknowledging that there is a problem but not yet ready or sure of how to make a change.
3. Preparing to make change.
4. Taking the necessary steps forward to make change.
5. Maintaining change.

The formal, theoretical process is known as the trans-theoretical model or stages of change. I've used these steps in my exercise psychology class and in training personal trainers for years but the process of change holds true for any change. The idea is that people progress through different stages of change on their way to successful change and at our own rate. Expecting that behavior will change by simply telling yourself to change is rather naïve (and perhaps counterproductive) because if it were that simple you would've already done it. Clients frequently come into a session and say, I know what to do but why am I not doing it? Because the process does not happen that fast. You can change the color of your hair or the style of your shoes in a day but you cannot change embedded thoughts, feelings or behaviors in a day.

One of the challenges in this process of behavior change is that people expect it to happen fast. A second challenge is that even when people say they are ready to make change, they are not quite ready. Many, unconsciously, want to hang onto their old behaviors (there are a variety of reasons). A third challenge is that people expect change to happen in a specific way, based on their perception. A great example of this comes from my work in exercise psychology. When people decide they should start an exercise (notice should) program, they think that they need to start off doing 1-hour everyday (notice the 1-hour, everyday) at the gym (the gym is not fun for most people). This is a good example (and one I see time and time again) of wanting change to happen quickly, wanting to unconsciously hang on to old behaviors and expecting change to happen in a specific way. This cycle sets you up for failure, guilt, pain, and a decrease in confidence.

People mean well when they want to move forward in this way but it doesn't work and it's not sustainable.

Story: earlier in my career I worked with a Weight Watchers group for a while. One woman really stood out to me. She had been trying to lose weight for years and was going to the gym but something just wasn't working for her. There were a few things that were working for her but the biggest problem was that she was going to the gym to work out and hated it. When I asked her why she did her exercise at the gym she responded, because that's what I thought I needed to do to lose weight. I asked her what other activities she liked to do. She responded with, "I like to rollerblade." I asked her why she didn't rollerblade instead of going to the gym. She said she didn't think that was considered exercise. I challenged her on this notion that rollerblading wasn't exercise and as her homework for that week I suggested that she get on the Internet and do some research on whether or not rollerblading was considered exercise. She came back the next week with a big smile on her face. She expressed how happy she was to realize that rollerblading really was exercise. She decided to quit the gym and start rollerblading again. A few weeks later during the group check-in my client shared that she had started rollerblading again and was starting to lose weight. Our perception is our reality but it's not always accurate.

Eventually, when you've been in the maintaining change stage long enough, you reach a point where you will be able to have clarity and work with your emotions, understand your own behavior and view it in an improved way. This can be considered transcending to a new way of thinking or behaving. In this stage, not only is your bad habit no longer an integral part of your life but to return to it would seem atypical, abnormal, even weird to you. You no longer need the old behaviors to endure and the new thinking and behaviors replace the old.

I am not sure I want to change

I hear ya'! Why rock the boat? You don't have to change. You can stay the way you are if it's working for you. If it's not working for you why wouldn't you want to change? Sure the old coping mechanisms may be safe, familiar, and comfortable but are they working? Change is what helps you to get to where you really want to be in your life. Is there a place that you really want to be but you struggle getting there? Either path is going to be bumpy but which path would you prefer: the one where you stay stuck or the one where you move forward? Which would you choose?

Making the choice to change

Change feels out of your control because you've been doing what you're doing for a long time. A situation happens, you automatically react and respond. You don't generally have to think about that. It just happens. Is that what you want to have happen? You have a choice to react and respond differently. The old coping mechanisms have been reinforced and once aware that they are not working changing them will take some time. It's important to understand that change is within your control. Without that realization there is no way to make change.

Defining successful behavior change

Successful behavior change is defined by you. When I talk with women about success I suggest that they move away from big markers as success indicators. For some of my clients the gold medal is a realistic success marker for them. That's a great goal to have if it's realistic but only one person gets the gold. It's important that there be smaller success moments on the journey to the gold. This helps my clients increase confidence and build motivation on an ongoing basis. It's important to not only have outcome goals but small, realistic goals that you're able to meet along the way that help you to feel successful.

Recap

As a kid you learn how to deal with things that are happening in your environment. The ways that you learn to deal with things as a kid tend to lose their effectiveness as you become an adult but these coping mechanisms tend to follow us for several years if not our entire life. For the coping mechanisms that work, this is great. For the ones that don't work, this can be a problem for you in achieving peak performance. It's time to ask yourself, "what is getting in the way of me reaching my goals" and become ready for the answer.

Stop

Ask yourself the following questions:

- As a child, how did you cope with things that were happening in your environment?
- Currently what is not working for you?
- What stage of change would you select?
- Honestly how ready to make change are you?
- How ready are you to go patiently through the stages?
- What small success indicators can you use today and tomorrow to help keep you motivated?

Chapter 5: Awareness - what's getting in your way (From Here...)

"I went to see Dr. Michelle because I'm an athlete that had some mental roadblocks that were preventing me from performing at my best. I was amazed at how it not only helped me in sports, but also how it transformed my life in everything that I do. This kind of change is so deep because it's work that you can do for yourself once you learn the techniques.

There were several things we worked on but what made the most impact for me was Dr. Michelle's guidance on awareness. When we become aware of what we're doing and aware of our environment (sights, sounds, smells, touch) we can get more clarity on the task at hand. We're not focused on what happened in the past or what might happen in the future because we are here in this moment right now, with nothing else to focus on but that. This important lesson came with practice drills and baby steps but within a few months I was overcoming roadblocks that I thought were too big to overcome." Denise M.

Intro

The first step towards peak performance is awareness. Without awareness you cannot take action to making change. Identifying behaviors you want to change can be challenging. We do what we do and for most of our lives we have reasons for doing those things. There are several ways people identify behaviors:

- Some people are very quick to realize when behaviors aren't working and quickly make a change.
- Some people bump up against adversity with what they are currently doing and decide to figure out how to change it.
- Some people work to be more present and aware in everyday life so they know what behaviors are working or are not working.
- Some people continue doing things the same way their entire life without any awareness.

Using the chart, think about your dream goal in the area that you want to make change. Where are you now (here), where do you want to go (there) and how are you going to get there?

What am I doing now	1	
	2	
	3	
What do I want to do 1 month from now	1	
	2	
	3	
What do I want to do 6 months from now	1	
	2	
	3	
What do I want to do 1 year from now	1	
	2	
	3	
What do I want to do 5 years from now	1	
	2	
	3	
What is my long term goal	1	
	2	
	3	
What is my dream goal	1	
	2	
	3	

Manifestation

How does someone figure out how to be more aware in everyday life? There are several ways awareness comes about. On a larger scale, awareness presents itself through education, therapy and the socialization process. Education does not have to come in the formal sense but can also include information from books and other professionals. Other professionals can help people target and identify behaviors they want to change. For example, a personal trainer can help people define behaviors outside of fitness (better sleep, better work production, shorter work days, eating better, feeling better and fewer doctor visits) that they want to work on and help them get there. They can talk to a client about cardio for heart health and weight lifting for muscle strength but take it a step further by educating people on the psychological benefits of exercise, for example, a good night's sleep. A good night's sleep can lend itself to more productive days, leading to a shorter work day, better food choices, less illness and fewer doctor expenses. These behaviors are the manifestation of the change we want to make.

Let me explain what I mean about manifestation. Usually when we realize that something's not working for us or something's wrong we pinpoint the problem as the manifestation. We see the manifestation of it. For example, say you are not running as fast as you'd like to run. How to deal with that? You probably run longer, run faster and spend more time running. The physical act of running, though, is not the problem. The problem usually lies in what's behind the manifestation, in this case running. What are some of the reasons that you may not be running as fast as you can? There could be many things behind the manifestation: anxiety, doubts, fears and worries. When developing awareness, it's important to dig a little bit deeper. You want to peek behind how the challenge is showing up. That is where you can make change. Working longer and harder is not usually the solution but working smarter is.

A level below manifestation

Awareness comes in many different forms. As stated above, an easy form of awareness is being aware of the manifestation of what's not working: not exercising, not eating right, not running fast enough, and not getting projects done. What's harder to be aware of is what's behind the manifestation. I like to call this mental and emotional awareness. In mental and emotional awareness there is macro-awareness and micro-awareness. Macro-awareness is the big picture. For example, I am not running fast enough because I lack confidence to go faster. Micro-awareness is the why, how and when; it's the specifics.

Story: a golfer I work with was struggling to improve his golf game (manifestation). When we drilled down we found that he was struggling with his golf game because he lacked focus and was dealing with anxiety playing with other people (macro-awareness). We developed his awareness around those situations where he is not focused, has anxiety and is not playing well (macro/micro-awareness). Now what? Now my client has to develop awareness of the moments when things are happening (micro-awareness). I teach him how to be proactive and think about situations be-

fore they happen so that he can adjust from what normally happens to what he wants to see happen. My client is driving to the golf course and instead of letting his mind wander as it normally does he now 'sets up the situation.' He is playing golf with a bunch of guys who are competitive which he knows produces anxiety for him. Furthermore, he knows that he is playing on a course that he's never played which produces even further anxiety for him. He consciously pays attention to his thoughts and takes notice of how those thoughts are affecting him physically. He now has the ability to develop coping mechanisms ahead of time for his thoughts and the physical manifestation of those thoughts in that moment.

It's been extremely important for clients to think about situations just before (so they have all the information) they go into them. It gives them a larger sense of control over a situation rather than getting in to a situation and allowing it to take over control. We determined when this kind of thinking was helpful. He needed those moments in his car on the way to the course and he needed those moments just before teeing off at the first hole (the first hole is generally a make it or break it for my client). While standing at the first hole before his turn, he is going to 'check the scene' noticing what's going on around him, what he is thinking and feeling and how that is showing up. This puts him in the moment and in control over the present situation where he can use the tools we developed for him to deal with those things that come up.

Get in the habit of reflecting

What does reflection mean? At the end of everyday take a couple of minutes to reflect (objectively and non-emotionally) on what went well, what you could have done better and a positive, surprise or something fun that came out of your experience. Why? It creates awareness and:

1. It is so important to think about what went well. We don't usually think in this way but it helps us recognize that we did do some things well, which is important for continuing to do well. It boosts confidence and helps us stay motivated.

2. What you could have done better. You will always remember what you didn't do well. As a matter of fact, we are trained to remember everything we didn't do well. Even if you don't write it down, you will remember. So why write it down? Writing it down gets it out of your brain so you don't have to carry it around with you.
3. A positive, surprise or something fun that came out of your experience. This again is aligning behind boosting confidence and motivation and it makes you feel good. ☺

I suggest writing your reflections out because it gets it out of your head and, in this case, it allows you to remember the positives surrounding the experience. If you keep track for several days, a week or a month you can go back and look at all of the positives, which continues to build motivation and confidence. Whenever I talk to clients about writing they tend to get squeamish. I am not talking about writing paragraphs of information unless that is what works for you. You can write words, bullet points or a few sentences.

It's your process and you should do it in whatever way feels comfortable.

You take the things that 'you could have done better' physically (triple lutz, free-throws, serve, or corners, for example) and mentally (like more confidence, less doubt, or more positive) and create a realistic action plan (goals) in any area of your life.

One way to develop awareness

I've never considered myself a very creative person but in my job I've had to get really creative with how I work with people. I actually love it. In my work, creativity flows out of me. In one of those creative moments I developed a way to help one of my clients become aware of thoughts and feelings. It is called a timeout. You do not need to sit in a corner for this exercise. ☺

1st progression

- Choose a time of day when you feel most mentally or physically exhausted.
- Set an alarm on your phone to go off at that time.
- When the alarm goes off, set another alarm for 1-5 minutes de-

pending on the amount of time you can take for a timeout.

- Start with body sensations: how is your body feeling?
- I have clients use progressive relaxation and breathing to relax the tension.

2nd progression

- Two timeouts a day.
- How is your body feeling?
- Additionally, what's your thinking?
- You may want to start writing it down.
- Work on connecting how your body is feeling to your thoughts.
- Work on changing any negative thoughts (more on this later in this chapter).

3rd progression

- All of the above.
- If your mind wanders gently bring it back to the exercise.

When you put a timeout in your schedule it becomes part of the day; a task, something you do. The alarm helps remind you to take a timeout and to think about how your body is feeling and where your mind is thinking (awareness). Writing it down reinforces the awareness. This begins to give you a deeper awareness, a connection with your body and a sense of control over being able to change what's been occurring automatically.

A more formal approach to developing awareness

I am going to walk you through one of the processes I use to help people develop awareness. Start by thinking about how much of what you are trying to attain is mental. Next, compare how much is mental with how much time you spend developing mental skills. Generally, most people know that everything we do is mentally demanding, yet they spend no time developing those skills.

Now that you understand that much of what you are trying to attain is mental and how little time you spend developing and working on your mental skills, let's figure out how to take action. Use the **Mental Skills Worksheet** below to determine what mental skills you think are necessary for you to be successful.

- Circle all the mental skills that apply and add any that aren't there.
- Narrow all those you circled to your top 5.
- Write your top 5 in order of importance on the **Performance Profile**.

Positive Attitude	Relaxed	Confidence
Concentration	Excited	Anger
Focus	Sportsmanship	Aggressive
Motivation	Pumped up	Decisive
Dealing with Anxiety	Courage	Reflective
Fear	Teamwork	Awareness
Calm	Disciplined	Dealing with Pain
Ability to Lose	Ability to win	Ability to Deal with Criticism
Handling Mistakes	Honesty	Having Fun
Sense of Accomplishment	Having Goals	Mental Toughness
Intensity	Acceptance	Respect
Consistency	Competitiveness	Loyalty
Enjoyment	Development	Humility
Control	Perspective	Balance
Intelligence	Being Present	Relentlessness
Self-esteem	Achievement	Adaptable
Communication	Positive Thinking	Dealing with Emotions
Drive	Resilience	Manage Pressure
Stress Management	Ethical	Intuition

Mental Skills
1.
2.
3.
4.
5.

Performance Profile

- Across the top of the Performance Profile is a rating scale of 1-10. Number 1 means "not at all" (For example, I am not at all positive) and 10 means "very much" (For example, I am very positive). To be most effective, bring colored pencils or markers, and have some fun.

- First, decide where you are currently in each of the five mental skills listed. Choose a color for "current skill level" and put an X in the corresponding box. For example, if you are feeling pretty positive, you might put an X in box 8.

- Second, decide where you want to be to succeed. Choose a color for 'success' and put an X in the corresponding boxes. Using the example above, although you are currently an 8 on positivity you may feel you need to be a 10 to excel.

- Third, use another color to draw a line between the X where your "current skill level" is and the X where you think you need to be for "success." This determines the difference between where you are to where you want to be.

This process will give you an idea of what you consider your mental skill priorities and give you awareness of what you need to work on to be suc-cessful.

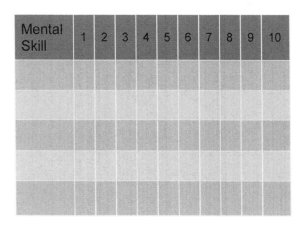

Mental Skill	1	2	3	4	5	6	7	8	9	10

Recap

Awareness is the key to making change. Without it, how would we know we want to move forward with making change? After becoming aware that something is not working, the next level is looking behind the manifestation of the thing you want to change. The thing is easy to be aware of but what's deeper than that becomes a little bit more challenging to figure out. It's important to drill down through the levels of awareness from macro awareness to micro awareness. Micro-awareness is where change becomes difficult but permanent. As you are able to make macro and micro changes you no longer have to work longer or harder but can work smarter.

Stop

Going through the above exercise gives you some mental goals to strive toward. Since you can't possibly work on everything at the same time, and more than likely you have not worked on any of them prior to this, start with the first one on the list. Using the example above:

- How do you get from an 8 to a 10 in positivity?
- Perhaps at an 8, you feel challenged with negative self-talk during certain pressure situations. What does that look and feel like?
- How does it play out?
- How does it affect performance?
- Delve deeper with into why you feel you are an 8 on positivity. This will help you figure out how to move past where you are and get you to the 10 you need to be.

Chapter 6: Dealing with the 'it'

Intro

In my practice there are five barriers that women struggle with: lack of resiliency, lack of confidence, negativity, lack of motivation and lack of focus. These seem to be the top five mental states of macro-awareness that get in the way of most women reaching peak performance and truly succeeding. These don't always show up in all areas of life but these are the top barriers that get in the way of what women really, truly want. Not having or knowing to develop these skills is what keeps women from making more money, getting bigger jobs, gaining recognition, and taking over the world; seriously.

1. Resiliency

"I met Dr. Michelle when she spoke at a community lecture on bouncing back from injury. As a runner sidelined by injury, I found her talk encouraging and helpful. She had a down-to-earth style, was very approachable, and obviously knew her stuff. I became an immediate

fan and subscribed to her Mental Moments blog. It was one of her posts that resonated with me and prompted me to reach out to her. Although I've always identified myself as being an intense perfectionist and overachiever, I've also harbored feelings of "faking it" and "not being good enough," which I believed affected my ability to advance in my career. When I emailed Dr. Michelle, I was ready to take a chance and make a change.

Dr. Michelle has a process that works. Sessions with Dr. Michelle are productive, actionable, and, many times, enjoyable. Her insights helped me to discover that what had been holding me back were negative beliefs about myself that I had grown up with, and she helped me to replace these with new beliefs about myself that were both positive and better resonated with me-- an endeavor that I was very skeptical about. In time, I had to admit even to myself that with each small success, I began to trust in her process *and truly believe in myself and my abilities. In a matter of months, not years, I was feeling SOLID self-confidence, learned better ways to handle emotionally charged situations without getting wrapped up in the emotions, and had a toolbox of proven strategies for tackling other situations that had been triggers for anxiety and self-doubt. Although I went to Dr. Michelle for what I thought was for purely professional reasons, the changes in my perspective and beliefs have benefited all aspects of my life. It's been about a year and a half since I first emailed Dr. Michelle and, while she doesn't think I need to, I continue to see her periodically, just to keep myself 'on track.'"*

L.B.

Resiliency is your ability to shrug something off and move on. It's your ability to let go or let be. Resiliency is important to have because otherwise you're always living in the past; trying to figure out what you could have done differently or how to fix something that's already happened. Resiliency is what gives you the ability to let go of something that has already happened. This enables you to be more present and more focused on what's currently happening so that you're able to act and respond to your present-day situation.

Lack of resiliency keeps you frozen in the past. It contains anxiety, anger, fear, frustration and can sometimes leave you feeling sometimes slightly depressed. It leaves you feeling defeated because you can't go back and change what's already happened but you are stuck in that space. It also leaves you feeling out of control because you don't have any control over what's already happened. Lack of resiliency shows up in thinking and also shows up in your body as tension.

Resiliency consists of not only getting caught up in the past but the future. As humans we tend to get so caught up in *should have*, *what if* and negative thinking that it consumes us. When these thoughts consume us we can't get done what we need to and we can't focus on the task at hand. When you are thinking about *what if* (I screw up that presentation) and are dealing with negative thoughts (I don't deserve to give this presentation), this can be detrimental on many levels. Although there are many ways to deal with this, clients really like the ability to question whether or not they are in control of the situation they are thinking about.

Here's an exercise: when you are thinking about a situation ask yourself if you have any control. This triggers your brain on whether or not it makes sense to be thinking about it and if it does, guides it into action. If you don't have control, your only option is to let it go (and continue to let it go as it keeps popping up). If you don't have control, figure out how much control (partial or full) you have and move forward.

The control gauge allows you to take control of *what if* and negative thinking and release it if it's not in your control. It also builds confidence and self-esteem and frees you to focus and use your energy in the present moment where you need it. You can use it today and feel the benefits immediately, as is the case with the client story below. My client used the control gauge and in one week began feeling free, in control, and happier.

Story: A client was struggling with what if *and* should have*. She utilized the above exercise and here's the result: "It's a breath of fresh air and I feel so much more in control, as I know that I have control over myself. I am so much better and happier and freer and feel wonderful when I let go of other peoples' actions and focus on what I can control – me. I also realized how much my internal dialogue was not productive and decided to cut it when it's not and also replace it with affirmations or what I'd rather be thinking or simply it's not in my control. Let it go."*

Daily exercises for building resiliency

These **process** exercises are designed to help you understand that when you stay focused on the process, you don't miss steps, have control and are ready for anything. Try one at a time and see which one works best for you.

The mechanics of cooking

Write out the entire mechanics of cooking your favorite dish.

- *What happens if you miss a step?*

94

- *What happens if you are thinking about the something else while you are cooking?*

Destination

- *If you were behind the wheel of a car (real or video game) do you focus solely on the destination? How do you get to the end or destination?*
- *If you were completing a project (work or school), do you focus solely on the end? How do you get to the end?*

2. Confidence

"Confidence is one of the most important mental tools that a person can have. Without confidence, it makes it hard to achieve what you want in life.

Dr. Michelle Cleere helped me to find my confidence again and overcome the mental challenges that were preventing me from achieving my goals. She gave me to tools to recognize the things that I could and couldn't control in my life. That gave me the confidence to take control of my aspirations and not let anything get in the way.

Dr. Michelle Cleere is to the mind what Muhammad Ali is to boxing. She has perfected ways of helping you overcome your mental challenges."

Lanny Barnes, 3-time Olympian

Confidence is important because it's your ability to meet the task at hand. If you feel like you're unable to meet the task at hand then you're going to feel a lack of confidence and a sense of defeat. The sense of not being able to do something then leads to a lack of motivation, anxiety and your inability to do it.

Confidence is a state of being. State means the condition of a person under certain circumstances. For example, you might be really confident on a 6.2-mile, easy training run but in a 6.2-mile race, not so confident. If you are running the same distance, what's the problem? In the first example, you are running 6.2 miles at an easy pace. In a 6.2 mile race you are running with a lot of other people and are more than likely racing for a specific time (not an easy pace).

I either have it or I don't

In the above example you are confident in some situations (state) and not others. For example, as an athlete you may be confident in practice but not so confident in competition. Or, you may be confident in your athletic abilities in your sport but not at all in another sport. Most people have confidence in certain areas or states but not in all and sometimes not in the areas they most want it. Why? When you really want something, you put a lot of pressure on yourself to obtain exactly what you want and nothing less. In those situations the increase in pressure leaves you feeling like you aren't confident. That may be the case and it may be the case that underneath all of the other obstacles getting in the way, there is a confident you.

I've talked quite a bit about state confidence; confidence in certain situations. In some fairly new research it has been determined that we also have traits confidence. Traits confidence is the amount of confidence that we are born with. Some of us are born with higher levels of confidence than others. Let me explain this in a different way. Some of us are born to be 25% confident. That does not mean that we can't increase our ability to be confident it just means that we start off at a lower level of confidence than an Olympian who is born with, say, 75%. I see this with elite athletes. Even though they hold the belief that they can perform at high levels they still have self-doubts.

How confidence is affected

Probably by most everything, if you let it! There are external distractions: environment, competition, coaches, teachers, family, friends, instructors, judges, critics, and spectators, for example, and there are internal distractions, like anxiety, self-doubt, worries, fear, and negative self-talk. In low pressure situations you might exhibit one or two of these distractions at a low level and those things could help facilitate a good performance. As pressure increases the number of distractions and the level of disturbance from them continues to increase. Distractions are called distractions for a reason. They distract you from your goal. Not only do they distract you but they detract, causing your attention and your energy to be taken in a completely different direction rather than taking you in the direction necessary to reach your goal.

Building confidence

One way to build confidence is to keep external and internal distractions in check. You also want to ensure you have realistic goals and trust the steps you are taking to meet those goals. Some other ways are as follows:

- Control--the control gauge is particularly helpful with external distractions. Ask yourself if you are in control of the distraction. If you are not, let it go.

- Act confidently--acting confidently helps you to think confidently and visa versa. Ask yourself what it would look like to act confidently. What do confident people display?

- Think confidently--self-fulfilling prophecy: if you are thinking confidently and positively, positive confident outcomes will follow. When you were at your most confident, what where some of your thoughts and what was the outcome? When you were at your least confident, what were some of your thoughts and what was the outcome?

- Talk confidently--how do you talk to other people about what you do?

- Think about successes--think about success in terms of successful moments. Keep track of them and feel good about them.

- Using imagery--see yourself doing things you've never been able to do or have had difficulty doing.

There is more to confidence than this but these are some key things to consider. Be aware of what gets in the way of your confidence, develop the ability to build confidence to combat the things that get in the way, and utilize other tools to build your confidence. Confidence is in your control.

Daily exercises for building confidence

These **confidence-building** exercises are designed to help you understand what confidence feels like and help you develop daily practices to strengthen it. Try one at a time and see which one works best for you.

Walk the Walk

1. Walk tall
   - *Shoulders back*
   - *Head high*
   - *How does this feel?*
2. Slouch
   - *Slump shoulders*
   - *Hang head*
   - *How does this feel?*

- *What the difference between the two?*

Daily Inventory

- *At end of each day, write down three to five positive or success-ful moments.*
- *Do this for a week.*
- *What do you notice about your sense of confidence?*

Role Model

- *Identify someone who does what you do that you look up to. Watch them: who they are and how they do it?*
- *How do they exhibit confidence and positivity?*
- *When you are facing challenges, ask yourself what your role model would do.*

3. Negativity

"I first came to Dr Michelle after years of doubting myself and my capabilities in my sport. I had had coaches over the years who I allowed to reinforce my negative thinking and while they pushed me to work harder and achieve more, I believed less and less in myself. Without totally knowing it, I created a negative thinking pattern which kept me from feeling good about myself, my goals and my own potential. I was damaged from the past, fearful of the future and stuck in an uncomfortable place.

In our first meeting, Dr Michelle asked me the hard question that I was too afraid to ask myself; she wondered what I thought was so wrong with me that I couldn't achieve greatness? Her approach was gentle and we got right to getting to the root of my insecurities. We went way back to some of my earliest memories and uncovered where my pattern of self-doubt stemmed from. I remember when Dr Michelle first told me that I have a perfectionist mentality and in each performance I would judge myself so harshly if it didn't go as perfectly as I wanted it to. Since my expectations were on things mostly out of my own control, I had no idea how to confront my fears and insecurities; I was a prisoner of my own negative mind.

Dr Michelle gave me so many tools and exercises to begin to retrain my brain. One lesson that has had the strongest impact was about objectivity and not adding anything to my performance or my practice. In the past, I would judge myself based on if something went good or bad, which often left me doubting myself and feeling like I had failed. Instead, Dr Michelle encouraged me to look at the situation with an objective eye. I have learned, and continue to learn, how to live more in the moment of the performance, how to share the performance with my audience, rather than be stuck in my own mind about it. This really helped me to see the bigger picture, to free myself from judgment and open my eyes to a new world of happiness and acceptance. In the end, I was thinking negatively over a past performance, bringing that negativity into each new situation, only reinforcing my own doubts and fears. Dr Michelle helped me to catch the moment this would happen, *stop it from happening and to become more present.*

Dr Michelle changed my life and has helped me to tackle some of my magic thinking habits. I'm so grateful that I have her in my life as my mental coach."

Eve Diamond, Circus artist /Aerialist

The #1 challenge is negative self-talk. Negative self-talk is a form of internal criticism and includes *should have*, *what if*, over-analyzing and choking. Negative self-talk is self-defeating, is counterproductive and produces anxiety.

When you have an experience that you perceive as more demanding than what you think you're capabilities can manage, you develop anxiety. The cognitive part of anxiety is negative self-talk. This anxiety leads to negative thoughts that lead to stress typically in the form of worry. Worry occurs when there is a discrepancy between what you hope will happen and what you perceive is occurring or will occur. Before you know it, you are unable to move or think clearly and are stuck in a down-ward spiral.

Self-fulfilling prophecy

- Negative self-talk leads to nega-tive things happening, like in golf "I am going to shank the ball" or in tennis "I am going to have a low first serve percentage."
- One negative thought leads to another which hinders perfor-mance because it also brings about tight muscles, shallow breathing, increased heart rate, and other physical symptoms of anxiety.
- Catastrophe theory--as negative cognitive thoughts continue, you continue to spiral out of control. Some people cannot regain their composure to keep moving for-ward. This leads to dropout and loss.
- Your body moves in the direction of your thoughts. If you are think-ing you can't, then you probably won't.

Becoming more positive

I absolutely believe that positive thoughts breed positive outcomes. As of late, I've taken a little bit of a different stand on positive thinking. For years I've worked with clients to change negative thoughts into positive thoughts. I know how detrimental the negative thoughts can be and how incredibly powerful the positive thoughts are. However, for some clients moving from a negative thought orientation to a positive thought orientation is way out of reach. I was asking them to go from one end of the continuum to the other. What ends up happening is that they end up feeling like they've failed because they can't quite get there. Feeling a sense of failure, they lose confidence and self-esteem and go right back to their negative orientation. Many of these clients also see things in black or white. Rather than keeping them in black and white thinking (negative to positive) I work to keep them out of the negative thinking but move them toward positive slowly so that the change is gradual. This is what I call neutral thinking. For example, instead of going from *I can't do this* to *I can do this*, I work with clients to find thinking that's gray or neutral, for example, *it's going to be hard but I can do this.*

There needs to be degrees of thinking rather than thinking that is all or nothing, black or white, win or lose. This thinking is designed for immediate failure. If you can't get all the way to the other side, why bother. Many of my clients have lost before they've even begun. It's much easier for them to go back to their negative orientation because it's familiar. Why trade familiar for failure and disappointment. The good news is, clients don't have to when that change is more gradual and realistic.

Tips for reducing and overcoming negativity

Thought stopping is the process of ceasing negative thoughts and replacing them with rational, positive beliefs. This technique prevents people from dwelling on nonproductive thoughts and helps you focus on the job at hand.

- Identify a particular negative statement you make in a particular situation, for example, before getting on the tee or on the court,

I often say to myself "What if I can't keep up?"

- Specify a term of cue you will use as a signal to stop your negative thoughts and move into the direction that you are trying to go, for example, say *strength*, take a deep breath, and hit your shot.
- You can also learn to replace the negative thought with a realistic, positive and constructive self-statement, like, "I've been training and there's no reason why I will not do well" or "it doesn't matter whether or not I can keep up. I'm going out to do my best. I can achieve this by staying present and focused on the moment."

- Think fun – people who are highly skilled have a sense of enjoyment and fun. Most of them look forward to the challenge of pressure situations.
- Breathe – breath control produces energy and reduces tension. If you are focusing on your breath you can't be thinking negatively.
- Use positive key words or phrases – saying and thinking

personally generated, positive words or phrases can be energizing and activating. Some examples are: *I can do it*, *push to the top*, *strong*, *fast*, or *tough*.

- Use imagery – imagery helps generate positive feelings, energy and feelings of success. It involves visualizing something that energizes you when you need energizing or slows you down when you need to be calmer. A tennis player might imagine placing a serve or hitting cross court while a golfer might imagine a perfect 160-yard shot from the tee or making a 15-foot putt.

Daily exercises for building positive self-talk

These **positive thinking** exercises are designed to help you change your thought patterns to be more positive. Try one at a time and see which one works best for you.

Bedtime routine

- *Envision yourself speaking and acting positively about the situation.*
- *Envision yourself doing 'it' well (having fun, with ease)*
- *Do this every night before bed for a week.*
- *What do you notice?*

Wake-up routine

- *Start your day with a positive word, phrase or affirmation related to the situation.*
- *Do this every day for a week.*
- *What do you notice?*

Pocket affirmation

- *Put a positive word, set of words or affirmation related to the situation on an index card and put in a pocket or bag.*
- *Refer to this card at the start of each day and two other times per day.*
- *Do this every day for a week.*
- *What do you notice?*

4. Motivation

"Several of my clients have used Dr. Michelle's services when they got "stuck". Mental ruts may be the toughest to overcome and Dr. Michelle has the tools and experience to help guide us through."

Stephanie Atwood, M.A., Founder/CEO
Go WOW Living

Motivation can be defined as the direction and intensity of one's efforts. Direction refers to why a person may be involved in a particular situation and why a person avoids other situations. Intensity is concerned with how much effort a person gives toward reaching a certain goal.

Many times when someone decides to do something, they may appear to be motivated. They do all the right things. The energy to move forward appears to be there. Why doesn't it happen? This happens because they are not mentally prepared. Having some knowledge in motivation will help you be able to understand certain behaviors and help you figure out how to motivate

112

yourself when you seem to be struggling.

Problem: a woman is struggling with motivation to exercise. Why? She didn't grow up exercising and it was not a family value. Solution: attach exercise to her values, find some form of exercise she loves, set small realistic goals and help her recognize when she's meeting them.

We get frustrated with ourselves for not being motivated and in some situations others see this lack of motivation and they get frustrated viewing it as an imperfection. We aren't aware of what's behind our lack of motivation so how can other people know? Don't judge yourself or others for something you don't understand, motivation is a great example. People see a lack of motivation as laziness until they are able to look behind it and realize its fear, anxiety, or lack of confidence. That can completely change the way you think about it.

Intrinsic versus extrinsic motivation

It's important to understanding that there are two types of motivation:

intrinsic and extrinsic motivation. Each form of motivation has a different impact. Someone who is intrinsically motivated does what they do for the sheer fun, pleasure and enjoyment of it. They are motivated by skill improvement, the inherent challenge of the sport and the achievement of personal performance goals. They are involved because they love it. Alternatively, people who are extrinsically (externally) motivated may do something for social approval, material rewards and social status. Extrinsically motivated people tend to believe that rewarding a behavior increases the probability that the behavior will be repeated and punishing a behavior decreases the possibility that it will be repeated. However, once a need is satisfied, it is no longer a goal and loses its power to reward. The more extrinsic rewards a person gets, the less need there is for the same type of reward.

Building motivation

When attempting to build your motivation it's important to consider the following list of things when dealing with motivational challenges:

- Understand why you are doing what you are doing.
- Clarify your expectations.
- Break things into small, realistic chunks.
- Set realistic goals. Goals provide opportunities for success.
- Ask for positive reinforcement from others and learn to give it to yourself.
- Be a part of the process of decision making.
- Incorporate fun and enjoyment.
- Place emphasize on the process rather than the outcome.
- Assess and correct inappropriate perceptions of yourself and what you do.
- Find successful moments.

Daily exercises for building motivation

These **motivation building** exercises are designed to help you become aware of what motivates you.

Make a list

- Write down all the things you love to do.
- Write down why you love to do these things.
- Write down all the things you do that you don't like doing.
- Write down why don't you like doing these things.
- *What do you notice?*
- *What do you feel?*

Break it down

- Take something you love doing and break it down to its core.
- What's there?
- How do you get to the end product?
- Take something you struggle with and break it down to its core.
- What and who do you need to be to get it done?
- *How can you take your process for getting to the end of doing something you love and use that in situations where you are doing something you don't love?*

Think success

- At the end of the day, get into the habit of writing down 2-3 successful moments.

5. Focus

"Working with Dr. Michelle Cleere to prepare for a Firearms Instructor Bull-seye Shoot-off competition was invalua-ble. Dr. Cleere counseled me on ad-dressing the mental challenges of shoot-ing and guided me to a deeper level of focus that helped to mute the external distractions, internal static and self-doubt. In that focused state of mind, I could truly concentrate on the process of shooting, not the results. Dr. Cleere helped me to see that it is in the process where I have true control and where the actual fun of the competition lies."

Natalie Arnold, Law Enforcement Officer

Take a walk in the woods. While you are walking focus on the sights, sounds and smells of what's around you. While you are washing dishes, ex-perience the texture of the soap on your glasses, plates and silverware. While cooking, focus on the textures, colors and tastes as you prepare the food. Have you ever missed a rare bird while walking in the woods, accidentally bro-ken a glass or burnt something on the stove? Much of this occurs because you aren't being present; in the moment. It's important to be present with whatever you do so that you have control and can act and respond appropriately.

Focus means learning what needs your attention, being in the moment with whatever needs your attention and being able to shift your focus to the next important thing that needs your attention.

Your focus is similar to a camera lens: the center is the sweet spot and around the sweet spot is the periphery. Your attention should be on the sweet spot and not the blurry periphery. However many people get caught up in the periphery where most distractions are negative which send them spiraling out of control. That is why they are called distractions. Your brain is overloaded with information that doesn't have anything to do with the task at hand and it shuts down. The good news is you can learn how to improve your focus.

It's one thing to be able to focus in everyday life but it's another thing to learn to be focused when pressure increases. An increase in pressure usually brings with it an increase in negative thoughts, worries, and self-doubt. In that place, you are overloading your brain with information and your brain goes tilt. How do you regain?

In either situation if you can give your full attention to the present moment it's not only energizing but it enables you to control your current reality. If in any given moment you are focused on the past or the future, what happens to that current moment? It's lost and then it becomes part of the past. Suppose you are lost in fear of your current interval workout: I hate this, I don't think I can do this again, this is going to continue being painful, there is no way I can do this. Because you weren't paying attention, the treadmill sped up and you fell off the back. If you had stayed focused on the moment, you would have been able to react in this situation. Because you were focused on something other than the moment you took a situation you were in control of, lost that control and gave it to something else. In this situation, focus not only ceased this workout but maybe future workouts. Your lack of focus fed into what you were thinking. This is called self-fulfilling prophecy.

You may not have realized this but you need to have the ability to change focus. There are different levels of focus depending on the situation. We have broad, narrow, internal, and external focus. Many situations require that we have the ability to not only recognize this but understand how to switch from broad to narrow (and vice versa) and from internal to external (and vice versa).

How we lose focus

There are internal distractors and external distractors of focus. Internal distractors come from within. They are the thoughts and worries that distract our focus from the task at hand. External distractors refer to environmental stimuli that divert attention from the important cues relevant to what you are doing. The external distractors include visual distractors (other performers) and auditory distractors (cell phones, music). Distractors increase as the demand increases and the pressures are more intense.

Refocusing

We all get distracted from time to time but the key is how efficiently we bring ourselves back to the present moment, how we refocus. The first step to refocusing is awareness. Be aware when you lose focus. Once you realize you have lost focus you can develop a plan to refocus. I like to work with clients to hone their focus using mindfulness exercises like walking in the woods, washing the dishes, or tasting a lemon. There are many other great ways to help bring you back into focus using energizing words, positive phrases, your breath, and imagery.

Learning to refocus requires you to have a regularly consistent plan to prepare for and use during high pressure situations. It's important to get into the habit of refocusing all the time. Practice at work, at home, and in social situations. For example, while you are out with friends when you notice that you are no longer a part of the conversation, practice gently bringing your focus back to the present moment. You could also take a deep breath and use a word like *refocus* to trigger your brain to do something different than you would ordinarily do.

Discussion board client: *I have been working on my focus. I have been working on my affirmations and visualization; with CDs as well.*

I have been doing the concentration exercises on your site and can stare at the black dot for 4 minutes. The numbers chart…you got me! Not even getting better at that one!

The reason that 4 minutes is my goal is that I am training for the national track pursuit on Sept.9th. I want to do it in 4-4:10 minutes. It is hard to focus during the whole event. I can't picture the 12 laps without a lack of focus at some point.

I listen to visualization CDs at night. I try to see myself racing as well. For me I find it hard to see myself doing the whole pursuit. I get distracted with thought have tried hard to turn up the dial and see myself big and hear my breathing and see my skin suit etc. I can do that. Holding the thought is difficult.
Last week I had troubles at the track with focus. I was with another very fast competitor and her fast times were throwing me off even if I pretended they didn't.

Last night I went and this time when she was up doing her pursuit I did not watch.

I closed my eyes and with the sound of her racing I visualized that it was me. I did not want to hear her time nor did I want to know anything about what was going on. I could not help hear it from others which is fine. But overall I performed better myself. My focus was more on me.

I find that sometimes I just go out there and don't focus. I do it but I am not into it. My last 2km repeat on Wednesday was like butter. I was so focused. The pacing was epic. My legs felt so good and I was on. My speed was on and I was red lined at the end. That is how focus feels.

I race this Saturday night and with all the equipment. It will be a good test. I want the focus to be bang on. I want to be calm. I want to feel that butter feeling.

My whole like, my emotions are what take over. I can get overwhelmed with emotions in an instant and cry. I never liked this. When I get embarrassed, it happens which makes it more embarrassing!

Learning to control my emotions will make me a better athlete.

Dr. Michelle: *you are doing so well with this mental stuff; so give yourself some credit* 😀

There are 2 simple things I want to instill in you about focus: 1) when you are trying to use your focusing skills, instead of emphatically trying to get immediately rid of the negative thoughts, once you notice the negative thoughts, take note of them, maybe take a breath and then move back into what you are doing; present moment. Allow yourself time to recognize what's occurring and then move into the moment and 2) visualizing the race or course may not work for you.

Choose something that does work for you; something that makes better sense and something that better captures your attention. Obviously visualizing the race is good; however there are other things you can use: visualizing yourself cycling in an area you love or visualizing your best performance. Do either of these seem like they'd keep your attention? Any of these will take practice :-). Start with something that is simple and easy and once you feel a little more focused move into the tough stuff like your race.

Does that make sense? Does that help? I like how you closed your eyes and used the sound of your competitor's race as your own. You are figuring out what works and what doesn't. That's important.

Practice using focus

- Become efficient at refocusing. We all get distracted from time to time but the key is how efficiently we bring ourselves back to the present moment. The first step is gaining awareness of when you are unfocused. Once you realize you've lost focus figure out how to bring yourself back into focus once again.
- Practice focusing your attention on the process of forward move-ment. So many people get caught up in the past but you have no control over the past. You only have control over this moment.
- Play around with focus in the easy areas of your life. Focus is a challenge in difficult situations. If

you can learn to be focused in easier areas of everyday life it will transfer over to more difficult areas.

- Learn how to use imagery. Recall experiences where you felt and use those images to help focus you during current situations.
- Allow moments of purposeful distraction. Sometimes reverse psychology works. If you say to yourself I am going to focus and refocus as best I can throughout this meeting and then when I am done, I will allow myself some time to just think about everything else, you'd be amazed how the brain interprets that information.

We have varying degrees of focus but you can train yourself to develop greater powers of present moment attention. You can learn to focus and refocus to provide yourself with a mental environment that is consistent with where you want to be. You can learn to control a wandering mind that diminishes your outcome.

Daily exercises for building focus

These **mindfulness** exercises are designed to help you learn to stay focused on the present, not judge yourself for losing focus and to learn how to bring your focus back. Try one at a time and see which one works best for you.

Mindful music

- *Choose a piece of music that you like and know the words to. On a walk or jog put the piece of music on. When you've noticed you lost focus, gently and without judgment bring your focus back.*
- *Keep doing this exercise until you can get to the end of the song without losing focus.*
- *What did you learn?*

Mindful dishes

- *Wash a couple of dishes but focus on the smell of the soap, the feel of the dish and the sound of the water. When you've noticed that you've lost focus, gently and without judgment bring your focus back.*

- *Keep doing this exercise until you can get to the end of a sink full of dishes without losing focus.*
- *What did you learn?*

Recap

I once heard Gregg Levoy give a talk. I felt a lot of synchronicity with what he was saying and how that's similar to the way I work with my clients. Gregg talked about acceptance: the ability to accept what is: yes and no, black and white and everything in between. He also talked about intuition: the little voice that comes from your soul or your heart.

Acceptance is an important part of this conversation, because if not then what? You lose resiliency, confidence, the ability to be positive, motivated and focused. You get caught up in *what if*, *should have* and *why didn't I*. You can't go back and you can't be somewhere you are not. Acceptance helps release you from chasing, chaos, negativity, guilt, judgments, perfection and allows you to accept yes, no and everything in between. It places you on the offense and allows you to be open to whatever comes your way. It dramatically increases your ability to think, move and act; to be in control.

What is intuition? It is your unconscious collection of experiences. It's that voice inside our soul, our gut or our heart that intuits what we should do. It's the authentic self. It's the part of us that knows us, where we should be going and what we should be doing. Why don't we follow the guidance of that voice? Because we think our head knows best. Unfortunately the head is what screws us up and moves us many times in the wrong direction. Our head is what sends us mixed messages, negative messages and has us repeat the deadly patterns of the past. Our inner soul is what's authentic.

Should artists paint from their head or their heart? Should musicians play by thinking or feeling? I understand that feelings are scary and that if you are used to thinking about things then it's hard to listen to your unconscious voice but it is there for a very, very good reason. It is not what gets in the way; your head does. It's there to show you the authentic way.

Story: a client beats himself up for eating a bowl of cereal that he thinks he

*shouldn't have eaten; thinking and be-
havior that leads to another bowl of cereal. He ate the cereal. He can't take it
back. If he could find a way to refocus in
that moment, he could make a change.*

*The key is acceptance. The first bowl of
acceptance may not be enough. It might
take a second and third but at some
point the brain will go, "damn! I am not
getting the guilt that I need!" and it will
cave into acceptance and the cereal will
be history.*

Stop

Ask yourself the following questions:

- Do you have control of the
  past or future?
- What do you have control of?
- When have you felt the most
  focused?
- When have you felt least focused?
- *What's the difference between
  the two?*

Chapter 7: Develop a plan-start by setting goals (there)

Intro

Up to this point hopefully you've gained the following information:

1. You've learned why it's important to envision yourself getting it.
2. You've developed awareness around what skills you need to reach your goals or get the job done.
3. You've thought about the obstacles that get in the way and how to start developing them so they become strengths.

In this section I want to share the next steps for moving forward by talking briefly about how to create a plan for forward movement.

Goal setting

Take the top 5 skills you put in the performance profile and start setting goals for getting there. Goal setting is a process that involves assessing one's current level of performance; creating a

specific, measurable, realistic, and challenging goal for one's future level of performance; and detailing the actions to
be taken in order to achieve that goal.
Why is this important? *You can't figure
out where to go unless you have a
roadmap, otherwise you get lost. Dr.
Michelle Cleere.*

Long-term goals are made up of
many short-term goals. For example,
say you listed motivation as a (long-
term) goal. On the performance profile
your self-assessment was that you are a
2 in motivation but feel you need to be a
9. You now know that it's important for
you to set goals around becoming more
motivated.

Short term goals not only provide
a focused path, but also provide motivation and confidence. Short term goals
help to focus your attention on the now.
One key to setting short-term goals is to
narrow down goals to the ones that are
the most important so that you do not
get overwhelmed by too many.

SMART goals

When written correctly, goals allow you to see your successes, which
lead to increased motivation. To do that

134

the research suggests using SMART goals.

Specific (vs. general) -- A specific goal has a much greater chance of being accomplished than a general goal. It includes who, what, where, when and why. It provides something specific for you to focus on.

Measurable (performance vs. outcome) -- Establish concrete criteria for measuring progress toward the attainment of each goal set: how much, how many, and how will you know when it is accomplished?

Adjustable -- Goals should change as you reach them so that you continue and stay motivated. Some goals may be a little out of reach and need to be modified to something more realistic. Goals should be within your control, and if not, need to be changed.

Realistic (vs. unrealistic) -- To be realistic, a goal must represent an objective toward which you are willing and able to work towards. Be sure that every goal represents substantial progress. A little bit of a higher goal is frequently easier to reach than a low one. A low goal exerts low motivational force. The goal is probably realistic if you truly believe that it can be accomplished. Additional ways to know if the goal is realistic is to determine if you have accomplished anything similar in the past or ask yourself what conditions would have to exist to accomplish this goal.

Time based (long-term vs. short-term) -- A goal should be grounded within a time frame. With no time frame tied to it, there's no sense of urgency. Goals are meant to motivate your athletes, and are an indicator of progress. Goals can be written and should be reassessed. Reassessment can take place every day, week, month or year, as long as you are flexible and understand that goals will change as time passes.

Benefits of setting SMART goals

- Goals direct attention to important elements that help in making change
- You feel more in control
- You feel empowered
- You feel satisfied
- It builds self-confidence
- It increases focus
- It increases motivation

Common problems with goal setting

- A failure to understand how to set goals
- You set only outcome oriented goals
- Your goals are not realistic
- You set too many goals
- Not knowing which goals are the priorities
- You fail to adjust goals
- Lack of support

Alternative: I like SMART goals but the challenge I've found is that it, for some clients, it becomes a process that is cumbersome and can feel overwhelming. Because of this I've come up with several alternatives to setting goals. Here's one that has really seemed to work with several of my clients. Think about the 1 main area of your life you want to make change, for example, I want to be motivated to workout and every day, dump one very realistic goal into that area of change so that you feel successful. As you meet 1 very realistic goal in this area, you can try doing the same thing for other areas of your life.

Develop an action plan for how you will achieve your goals

This can be done by using the action plan template below which clearly spells out how you will achieve each short term goal. In order to achieve goals they need to be broken down into smaller bite size pieces. An action plan is the first step in breaking a goal down ever further. A few of the most important elements of the template I've provided are that it allows you to think about what needs to get done on a micro level, what resources you need, and what difficulties/barriers you might face in completing this objective.

ACTION PLAN				
GOAL:				
Today's Date:		Goal Completion Date:		
Objective (what needs to be done)	Resources needed (money/time/people)	Measurement of task completion	Target Date	Status
Possible Difficulties:				

From your action plan create a task list

A task list breaks things down even further from the goal -> action plan -> task list. The task list might include things like phone calls, scheduling meetings, writing emails, or research. Why is all of this important? This is how you reach your goals. I've always had goals but never used to break them down into smaller pieces. There are times I would miss a step. Sometimes I would get frustrated because reaching a goal was never as simple as I thought it should be. For example, if my goal is to write an article for a magazine, sitting down to write is not the only step I need to do to complete my goal. I need to decide what I want to write about. I need to do research on my topic. I may need to interview people. I need to decide what elements of my topic are relevant to my audience. When I started making an action plan and a task list, things became much clearer and less frustrating. Reaching my goal was a lot easier.

A task list that prioritizes the tasks in your action plan is a tried and true way of becoming more efficient and getting on top of what you need to do. A prioritized task list helps busy people get things done. It does this by helping you to:

- Remember tasks that have to be done.
- Organize tasks based on their priority.
- Estimate and allocate time for each task.
- Work towards your established goals.
- Think about what might get in the way of you completing you action plan.

Goal evaluation – staying focused and on course

Review your goals and the difficulties that you may have in reaching your goals regularly. Your priorities and circumstances may change, and it is important to be able to adjust your goals when things change.

You do not have to go through this process to be an effective goal setter. The most important things to realize are that goals are helpful particularly when set the right way and that breaking them into smaller pieces makes them easier to achieve.

Restructuring your new world

I've always worked mainly on mental states and emotions but have had to also include structure and tactics. I find that more and more clients need the latter. I still work with them on mental states and emotions but they need more support to make it happen.

Story: I've worked with a client for several months on the mental states and emotions around eating healthy, working out and losing weight but he's not been able to do it. We've talked about exactly what to eat and when to eat but it wasn't working so I realized I needed to take a slightly different approach to the situation.

We sat down with one week's worth of calendar pages, Monday – Friday. We talked about when he should eat breakfast and what he should eat. He listed out breakfast foods. We did the same thing for lunch. We did the same thing for snacks. We revisited our conversation about why snacks are important, how often he needs to eat a snack and why. Even though we'd had that conversation before, having it in the context of scheduling out his day brought a new awareness to him around why a snack at 10, 2 and 5 are important if he was eating breakfast at 7:00, lunch at 1:00 and dinner at 8:00.

We talked about when he was going to write the grocery list (the grocery list contained only items we talked about or recipes given to him from the nutritionist) and when he was going to go to the grocery store. My client rarely went to the grocery store. When he did go to the grocery store he never went with a list. He'd run into the grocery store when he had time which generally ended up being 15 minutes before he had to be somewhere else.

We talked about accountability. More specifically, how I could support him. Although we weren't able to finish that conversation I started sending him text messages to remind him to get groceries or check in to see how his eating schedule was going. He emailed and sent text messages back saying that things were going good. I had him talk to *his nutritionist and get a week's worth of dinners; not a recipe for one thing but full meals and only meals that require a few ingredients including portion sizes; both things have been a challenge for my client.*

This structure was a good starting place. It's been two weeks but this week my client and I plan to talk about what worked and what didn't work and add a couple more things to the structure. For example, what accountability does he need around food, meals and exercise? We will add dinner to the structure. We will add a realistic amount of exercise into the plan and also include times when he can take the stairs (versus the elevator) or take a walk around the office.

We will keep developing this plan a step or two at a time and refine the plan until it works! This will help increase motivation and build confidence.

It is as difficult to make these kinds of changes as it is to make mental state and emotional changes. Why? We don't know what we don't know!

Not only is there work to do to make the change itself, but you also have to restructure your life to accommodate that change. It won't fit into your existing structure and if you try to make it fit you are only setting yourself up for failure.

Tactics

Now you have to realistically figure out how much time is appropriate to participate in an activity regardless of what you've done in the past, chunk out that time and schedule it. I had a conversation with a client who used to be a competitive marathon runner. At one point after training and competing in several marathons, life got in the way and for 12 months he stopped training and competing in marathons. He's tried several times to come back but wasn't feeling motivated. Here are some of the reasons for that:

1. He was expecting his mind and body to be OK picking up where he left off. Running 60-90 minutes a day, 6 days a week at 6 minute miles.

2. Because of that he was setting himself up for failure every time

he ran. He would not be able to run 6 minute miles for 60-90 minutes, would stop 20 minutes into a run frustrated and go home. He got hurt trying to run 6 days a week.

3. He kept failing so after 6 weeks he stopped running again.
4. He began losing motivation to potentially ever do another marathon.

When you think about it in that order, it does make sense that he would lose motivation. This is a very common scenario. Even people who have never worked out or run a marathon have grandiose expectations of what they should be able to do and in a relatively short amount of time. I've worked with so many people who have this notion that when they start working out they need to start by doing 1-hour. Imagine never having worked out (or not having worked out much) and jumping in for an hour every day (setting yourself up for failure, stopping working out and losing motivation to ever workout again!).

Let's get real and be realistic. To start:

- Figure out how much time is realistic based on how much you've been doing.
- Figure out how much is realistic given your life (work, school, family, social time, etc.).
- Figure out where you have time in your schedule.
- Figure out what you can add into your day, like parking farther away, taking the stairs, cardio gardening/grocery shopping/house cleaning.

Now chunk time out in your schedule. For example,
- I have 10 minutes in the morning to do a few yoga poses.
- I have 10 minutes after I put the kids down for a nap to do cardio-house cleaning.
- I have 10 minutes to walk/jog/run.
- I have 30 minutes 2 times a week to go to the gym.
- I have 10 minutes in the morning and 10 minutes in the afternoon to do something.

You can also do this with food. For example,

146

- I am going to start drinking more water: I am going to start with 8oz a day (versus going for the big gulp 64oz amount).
- I am going to start eating more fruits: I am going to eat 1 fruit 3 x's a week (vary the amount for each and every day).
- I am going eat less sugar: I am going to split desserts or have 1 less dessert a week (don't go cold turkey--if you want dessert and deny yourself dessert it's all you will think about).

One of my clients has been struggling with eating healthy. There are numerous reasons for this but one of the biggest reasons was because he didn't understand that there were options and that he was in control of those options. For example, at lunch he always wanted the pasta but knew he should have the salad. He didn't realize that he could have a salad with some protein and a small portion of pasta versus denying himself any pasta. Every day he felt deprived. This journey is not all or nothing. There is a lot of grey area and it's important to find it.

I missed a day so why bother

So many people live in either black or white, all or nothing. Much of the conversation goes like this: "Well, if I can't do it for one hour, 7 days a week then I might as well not do it at all" and they give up. As a society, have we really evolved to this place of either 0% or 100%? Is that all there is? For example, a weight loss client has several of the mental and physical skills he needs to lose weight but unless he follows the plan 100% of the time he won't do it. Here are some problems with this:

1. In this space there is no room for mistakes. We learn from mistakes and mistakes give up feedback for improvement.
2. Some people don't do anything if they feel they aren't going to get the perfect outcome they desire.
3. Perfectionism comes with a price. It sets you up for failure 100% of the time.
4. Perfection is not realistic.
5. I've ask clients to define perfection and they can't.

6. I've asked clients where, for example, they've gotten the notion
   that they have to work out for one
   hour every day and they don't
   know.

It's important to think about what
might be in the grey area. There is a lot
between black or white, all or nothing,
perfect or imperfect but you probably
have not had the opportunity to think
about what that is. It's important to think
about what things might be realistic for
your life.

Moving into the grey matter

Trying to live your life, going back
and forth from black to white is a challenge. Think about it. You are going
from one end of the spectrum to the
other. More often than not you end up
feeling like you've failed because you
can't quite get to perfect. Failure leads
to a loss in confidence and self-esteem
and you go right back to what's safe,
comfortable and familiar even though it's
not working.
Moving into shades of grey
should be a gradual step. Here are

some things to think about using the above example:

1. How many minutes are in between 0-60?
2. How many minutes a day are you working out now?
3. How many days are in between 0-7?
4. How many days a week are you working out now?

There can be/should be degrees of thinking rather than your life being all or nothing, black or white, win or lose. Align your thinking so that the change is gradual and you are moving up the continuum towards your goals. This is what I call taking neutral action. For example, instead of going from I can't do this to I can (absolutely) do it, find in between thinking like, it's going to be hard but I can do this.

Recap

Change can hard because you remember the difficulty of making it happen, fitting it into your schedule and knowing what to do. Having goals and breaking them down into sizable pieces

make change more manageable because every piece builds confidence.

Breaking goals into pieces helps
you to realize that we have moments,
versus hours, days or weeks. Each
moment is a new moment. If you only
have 10 minutes of time to work out, it's
okay. If you eat an unhealthy breakfast,
it doesn't mean that you couldn't and
shouldn't eat a healthy lunch. If you
don't work out today you can work out
tomorrow. If the treadmill is on level 20
and it's moving too quickly, you can
slow it down.

Until you've had some successes
and build some confidence, missing a
day may be uncomfortable. It partly
goes back to black and white, perfec-
tionistic thinking but also has a lot to do
with fear. If I miss one day, I'll miss another day which will turn into a week and
then it will be difficult and challenging to
start over.

Once you gain experience with
what to do and what to expect, starting
over is not as difficult. Mental tools: understanding how to set manageable
goals and knowing how to schedule
things, help you to see things differently.
If it's hard to restart, don't stop. Start to
think about your life in terms of your

ability to have options and make choices. Once you start coming from this
place you will feel more in control of
whatever you choose to do. In this
space, if you miss a day you have the
option to start again tomorrow.

Stop

Ask yourself the following questions:

- How can you break your task
  down even further?
- What barriers might get in the
  way of you reaching your
  goals?
- How can you think about your
  task differently?
- Where can you find 10
  minutes?
- Where do you go every day
  that you could take the stairs?
- Where do you go every day
  that you could park a few ex-
  tra blocks away?
- Would working out two days
  instead of five be more manageable?

Chapter 8: Get the support you need

Intro

Social networks can strongly influence behavior and beliefs. People who are trying to change their behavior and who have strong social support fare better. That social support can include family, friends, coworkers, personal trainers, group exercise instructors and other people who provide encouragement, support, accountability, and company. Social support is one of the strongest predictors of adherence to change.

It is important to understand the amount and type of social support you may need. As you think about prior successes, think about the amount and kind of support you had. Were other people involved in your past successes? Did family and friends help support you? Who was the most important person that added to your success? Inevitably adherence and success can be partially attributed to social support. Not only is it helpful to think about past successful experiences but it's also helpful to think about past unsuccessful experiences. It is difficult for people to connect their

successful experiences to social support, just as it may be difficult to connect
your unsuccessful experiences to lack of
social support.

*Story: a client came to me struggling to
eat healthy, lose weight and maintain an
exercise program. He is married and
has kids but feels very alone and
doesn't feel supported in his endeavors.
Because he is either working or spending time with his family he doesn't have
friends. He had been on this journey for
quite a while and decided to get support
so he came to see me.*

*Originally he was happy living on this
island but he has come to realize that
one of the reasons change has been so
difficult for him is that he doesn't have
the social support he needs. Part of his
journey to make change was to figure
out what kind and how much support he
needed. He already had a personal
trainer. He and I worked on his mental
states and emotions and we realized
that he needed a nutritionist for support
with healthier eating. All of this support
has been helpful but still not quite
enough so he started taking cycling
classes and running with a group of*

guys from the gym and this helps him with motivation and confidence.

Some of my clients may have a strong social support network while other clients may have a limited number of connections. For clients who have a strong social support network it's important to help them figure out how to utilize the social support they have available. For clients who have a limited social support network or no social support network it's beneficial to help them fine the social support they need to adhere to change. There are usually several opportunities within reach to get social support but clients have a hard time accessing it or realizing it as support.

There are different kinds of support

I'll bet that when you hear the word support one thing comes to mind: "ah I need to find someone to help me." Maybe, but there are also other kinds of support you can get, for example, reading this book. ☺

Instrumental support

Instrumental support is the tangible and practical factors necessary to help a person adhere to change or reach their goals. Some examples include transportation, a computer, or a babysitter.

Components of instrumental support that are unsupported actually turn into barriers. People will not be able to adhere to change if there are tangible things that get in the way of them being able to carry it out. For example, if you don't have a working computer, how are you going to get work done? In today's society, it's really difficult to do much of anything without a computer.

Emotional support

Emotional support is expressed through encouragement, caring, empathy and concern. Getting praise for your efforts, encouragement to work harder and sympathy when things aren't going exactly the way you want them to, are all examples of emotional support. Emotional support enhances self-esteem and reduces anxiety.

Informational support

This type of support includes the directions, advice, or suggestions you get about how to make change happen and feedback regarding your progress.

Companionship support

Companionship support is probably the most familiar type of support. It includes the availability of family, friends, and coworkers to know about and support you in your endeavors to make change.

Companionship during change produces positive feelings and will help distract you from negative feelings such as fatigue, pain, and boredom. Companionship also provides a sense of camaraderie and accountability.

Support comes in different forms

These different kinds of support can come in different forms: family, friends, supervisor, group exercise instructors, books, videos, neighbors, networking groups, nutritionist, doctor, and many more.

Family

The positive effects of a supportive spouse or partner on change behavior has been consistently demonstrated. For example, healthy married adults who joined a fitness program with their spouse had significantly better attendance and were less likely to drop out of the program than married people who joined without their spouse.

There can be several downsides to family support. When family members pressure or make loved ones feel guilty, you may actually respond by not wanting to change. This is known as behavioral reactants. People generally do not like to be controlled by others and upon feeling pressured and controlled will do the opposite.

Family members may also provide a sense of guilt because the emphasis on change is taking away from family time and family obligations. Change in one family member's life also affects all of the other family members. That can be scary for other members of your family.

Exercise instructor

A group exercise instructor's job is to engage, connect with, and get to know the people in their class. The group exercise instructor should introduce themselves, ask and remember members names, acknowledge new class participants ensuring they are properly set up for class, introduce new class participants to veteran class members, talk to members about their goals and expectations, and check in with members after class.

A good exercise leader can have a positive social influence on people and can contribute to increases in self-efficacy, enjoyment, and motivation to exercise. Group exercise participants who experience a socially supportive leadership style reported the following:

- Greater self-efficacy
- More energy and enthusiasm
- More enjoyment of the class
- The ability to try new things
- Greater confidence

These results indicate that a socially supportive group exercise instructor can have positive effects on participants in a single exercise class which also contributes to an overall increase in life satisfaction.

Work environment

The research is clear that a sense of cohesion in a work setting is related to whether or not an individual does a good job. Some principles shown to increase group cohesiveness include the following: group distinctiveness, giving group members responsibilities for particular tasks, established group norms, providing opportunities to make sacrifices for the group, and increased social interactions.

There is some evidence to suggest that the characteristics of the people in a work environment can affect the experience. Some of the things that affect the experience are gender, assimilation, and enthusiasm.

The gender makeup of a work environment is one group composition factor that can affect your experience. Women often report feeling uncomfortable in an environment that is made up of primarily men.

Feeling similar to other group members in a work environment can affect comfort level and motivation. People would prefer to work in an environment with people of a similar ability. Feeling less competent can diminish self-confidence and motivation

In my experience with clients

My Olympic and professional athletes are high in trait motivation and confidence but continued family support is what helps them to excel well into their 30's. Parents make investments of tangible and intangible resources found to be essential in nurturing promising individuals with talent. Their parents provided financial support and transportation to numerous competitions and performances. They also provided considerable social-emotional support, facilitating disciplined involvement while avoiding excessive pressure and expectations. Most of the results clearly show that talent development is a long-term process that involves not only the talented individual but also a system of support.

For most of the rest of my clients, they have to figure what kind and amount of support they need to move through life and make change happen.

As is the case with everything else I've discussed in this book, support doesn't always show up in exactly the way you think it should or want it to and sometimes you have to work for it. Case in point, a client was struggling to get the support she needed from her supervisor at work. We talked about how the supervisor probably wasn't going to change which meant that she needed to take responsibility for making change. This change included managing up, asking more of the right kinds of questions, and asking for what she needed.

Recap

It is critical that you consider whether or not you require support and what kind of support you need. Some people may need companionship support while other people need instrumental support. Once you identify your support needs you can figure out where to get that support.

Stop

Some questions to ask yourself:

- Do you need support?

- What kind of support do you need?
- How much support do you need?
- Where do you get the support you need?

Chapter 9: Staying motivated to keep going

"There comes a point in every athlete's career when you realize that all the training in the world won't get you to that next level. This is the point when you realize that your mind is getting in the way of your performance. To get to the next level in my Olympic career I received the help of Dr. Michelle Cleere. My mental barriers were enormous, but Michelle helped me to break down those barriers and overcome the doubts I had about my ability. She gave me the tools necessary to overcome distractions, barriers, and setbacks and helped me excel in sport. Michelle also gave me the tools I needed to capitalize on my strengths making me a better, stronger athlete."

Tracy Barnes, Olympic Biathlete

Intro

Mental training has helped many of my clients reach peak performance and it can help you, too. I am starting this chapter with several client examples so you can see how they got from here to there.

Due to confidentiality I can't talk specifically about who my clients are but I can share some moments of success which are partly attributed to clients working on their mental states and emotions. I am going to share the experiences of three clients to give you an idea of what can happen when you develop the right mental plan for reaching peak performance.

Swimming for a triathlon

I recently found myself in the terrifying position of discovering I had "open water phobia" only weeks before my first triathlon. I had really become comfortable in the pool but in the open water I was experiencing panic attacks and inability to breathe (a little inconvenient!). Luckily, I got a referral to Michelle from a friend and she helped me ENORMOUSLY.

We did a few sessions in her office really exploring the details around what brought up this anxiety and it was calming and helpful. But when that stubborn phobia just didn't go away completely,

Michelle went Above and Beyond in a way that truly made all the difference: she offered to go IN the water WITH me to help me, breath by breath and stroke by stroke. That was the breakthrough for me – having someone calmly WITH me, in the deep water. It was incredibly re-assuring as she gave me practical phys-ical as well as psychological tools to deal with the situation. Two days later, I did my first blissful one-mile swim in the bay that felt effortless and awesome.

If I could give her ten stars, I would. It feels like nothing short of a miracle. My triathlon is this coming Sunday and I am facing it with excitement instead of dread.

If you have ANY issues with mental preparation around any sport, Michelle will you give you her 100%. She's amaz-ing! (Yelp review)

Professional tennis player

I started with a tennis player who had just turned pro. This player had been ranked #1 in college but turning pro was a rough transition. This player was struggling with a lot of fear, anxiety and confidence. It was showing up on the court. This player was used to being part of a team and partially attributed her success to the team environment and upon turning pro realized that it was all gone. She was struggling to find the motivation and confidence within to carry on.

We worked on coming up with a game plan for dealing with the mental challenges around her game: fear, anxiety, worries, confidence and leaving it all off the court. We worked on imagery, performance routine, a routine between every point, a service routine, simulation training, thinking confidently, and more.

In one year this player went from being ranked in the high 600's to being ranked in the mid 200's. There are still things this player needs to continue to work on to make it to the top 100 but she has a solid plan in place.

Professional musician

A professional musician came to see me after several attempts to win auditions. This musician was struggling with fear, anxiety, worries and confidence. The musician's type A personality brought with it extrinsic motivation and expectations that were colliding into burnout disaster every time an audition came around.

We spent a lot of time bringing awareness to when, what and how all of this was showing up and then talked about performance routines, imagery, positive cue words, confidence, tapering, reducing type-A behaviors and feeling rather than analyzing.

For the first time in her life, this musician has felt great going into auditions and has made it through to several final round auditions.

Keep moving forward

How do you keep moving forward with anything in your life? You can even think about it like this, how do you keep moving forward in situations that are hard or seem impossible? Everything in life has peaks, valleys and plateaus. Many of the things I've already talked about are designed to help you keep moving forward but the reality is that life gets in the way, change is hard and when something is hard it becomes less of a priority. Know and accept that this is going to happen.

Plateaus

Plateaus suck. Our bodies go from losing weight consistently to getting stuck at a certain number. We go from building muscle and getting stronger, to having a week or two where we can't seem to lift anything heavier. We are happier when we make progress. When we work hard for something and don't see progress, we get unhappy.

Plateaus are really just issues with concentration in disguise. Before you think you're stuck, or in a plateau, consider the following:

- Oftentimes you think you are being diligent, but are you?
- Has the initial luster of new-ness, progress and winning worn off and are you expect-ing more for less?
- Are you eating well?
- Are you sleeping well?
- How are you dealing with any stress in your life?
- Are you exercising?
- Are you feeling balanced?

Your progress at a constant, consistent pace will definitely slowdown at some point but when we are talking about change it's usually because change is happening or has happened and you don't need to be working at the same pace. This can feel like a plateau and you might need to slightly adjust your expectations.

Story: one of my clients made a lot of change in a relatively short period of time. We dug in, developed some awareness and she did the work that was necessary to move her forward. Every so often she'd come in for a session feeling as though she had plateaued but what was really happening is that she initially made a huge amount of change, didn't have as much work to do, so it felt like she'd stalled out. In actuality, she'd done the work but she was missing the adrenaline rush of making huge, consistent changes in her life.

Staying motivated

Story: Tricia came to see me because she was struggling to stick to an exercise program. It was hard for her to get motivated to workout. What helped her was to define exercise and find ways to incorporate simple, short spurts of exercise into her daily life. We did a lot of work around what type of activities she liked which moved her in the direction of Salsa dancing. We also discussed what types of support she needed to adhere to an exercise program and found some friends who also loved Salsa dancing. She started by putting x's on the calendar for the days she participated in Salsa dancing. It was initially pretty motivating for her. The first month she only had a few x's but it was enough to keep her motivated to keep going.

Each week we would talk about how she was doing and every month I would have her bring her calendar in so she could see how far she progressed from month to month. We talked about barriers and benefits. Every month she had more x's on her calendar.

After a few months she realized the x's on her calendar weren't motivating her as before. She wanted more information about how she felt, barriers, sleep, diet, and her emotions. She tracked this information on a chart. She started to see cycles around her sleep and food that *had a lot to do with how she was feeling. She developed a greater awareness around what was getting in the way of her ability to exercise. We developed a plan for dealing with barriers and emotions. She finally felt like she was in control. She was able to see the connection between her workouts and her ability to feel better. She felt stronger, less anxious, better able to deal with stressful situations, and she had more energy to get through the day.*

Self-monitoring

The example above is a form of self-monitoring. Self-monitoring is usually done in the form of a daily written record of the behavior that you want to change. This can have a variety of forms: journal, calendar, chart or graph. It is important for you to find an effective, individual method of self-monitoring. Include everything you think is important. The following are benefits of self-monitoring:

- It gives you the opportunity to look at progress over time.
- Being able to see progress builds self-confidence and self-esteem which leads to adherence.

- It can be used as a form of accountability. If you are going to show it to someone each week it can help keep you motivated.
- Self-monitoring encourages you to be honest which encourages you to stick to what you are doing.
- It serves as a reward.
- It helps you identify challenging situations and barriers.

Reflective Journal

At the end of each day, think back through the day and write down the following with regards to your goals:

- One thing that went well.
- One thing that didn't go as well.
- One new thing you learned that was fun or positive.

Cultivating this retrospective awareness will help bring you back to the moment so that you can better recognize what did go well, what your focus can be for the next day and that from change can come fun and positive experiences that you weren't expecting.

Adjusting goals

It is through self-monitoring that you become aware of how you are doing at reaching your goals. If you are seeing some success and continuing to feel motivated, then you are probably on track with your goals. If you are feeling unsuccessful and overwhelmed your goals might not be realistic and it's important to readjust them.

Through self-monitoring, Tricia realized that she needed support and accountability to be successful. For example, she realized hiring a personal trainer would help her to be a more consistent exerciser. She also hired a mental training coach who helped her work through her emotional attachment to food.

Self-management

Self-management refers to managing your behaviors, thoughts, and emotions. Self-management skills improve your ability to look at your behaviors, thoughts and emotions and to change whatever isn't working. It helps you cope with and adapt to lifestyle changes such as those associated with making change.

Effective self-management skills maximize self-control energy, channeling it into the most important areas. Self-management skills increase the likelihood that desired changes in behavior will occur. These skills help you change your environments in ways that support your adherence to making change and help you cope with difficulties that might otherwise short circuit plans.

Self-management skills are rarely taught and it is generally not until you've had an experience where you need them that you figure out how to get them. For example, some clients have the ability to talk themselves into making change even when they don't want to while others won't do it.

Recap

In chapter 4 I talked about how change takes approximately 6 months. During that period of time lots will happen: you'll be up, you'll be down and you'll be all around. It's change and it's hard. Not only is the change hard but the process is hard; it's unfamiliar and uncomfortable. The bottom line: Is it something you want? Obviously what you've been doing hasn't quite been working (working longer and harder) so it must be something else. I am not gonna lie, change takes persistence and perseverance. The way that you get those is through honesty, changing the way you see things and acceptance.

Stop

Ask yourself the following questions:

- How do you motivate yourself to keep going?
- What do plateaus look like in other areas of your life?
- How have you moved through other plateaus?
- What does a plateau mean about who you are?
- What self-monitoring tool do you already use?
- What self-monitoring tool would work in this situation?

Chapter 10 backwards - you can do this

Story: I once had a very skeptical client walk through my door. She was working with a therapist but wasn't feeling any better and couldn't imagine ever feeling any better or differently than she did in that moment. I vividly recall some of our first conversations where she'd say, yeah, um, not sure you can help and I am not sure I want to try but I will come in for one session. She'd come in and I could tell she was overwhelmed, frustrated and unsure. Initially she hardly ever made eye contact. She would cry and talk for a long time without stopping. I sat, looking at her, listening to her every word. Occasionally I would ask a question. She left many sessions not sure that she was coming back for another. Each week she let her guard down a little more. She started to make a little more eye contact. I would listen. I would ask more questions and I would listen.

There are moments in client relationships that I point out discrepancies or bring out an alternative perspective but the biggest part of my work is helping people find solutions for things. The solutions are not always for huge things but for very tiny things. Things we think about ourselves but are too afraid to say out loud, things that perhaps only someone such as I would surmise.

About 4-5 weeks into our relationship, I started making small, gentle suggestions for solutions. My client would come back the next week and say, thank you, that thing you said last week as I was walking out the door really helped. After several weeks of this, life was starting to shift but my client was still in that really hard middle place; afraid of going forward and terrified of going back. Here's what I did: I shared my life story with her. Someone videotaped one of my talks where I share part of my life story and I sent this to my client. This was the tipping point. In a relatively short amount of time her entire world has changed.

You can do this. You just need to understand that you can't keep doing things the way you are doing them for change to happen. To help, I am giving you three free gifts to support your continued work toward lasting change.

My Free Gifts to you

Thank you for buying my book From Here to There: a simple blueprint for women to achieve peak performance in sports and business!

Because you've bought my book you are eligible to receive 3 special gifts that no one else has access to:

1. Dr. Michelle's EZINE: "Getting What you Want"
2. The opportunity to apply for a *Confidence to Win* Breakthrough Strategy Session with Dr. Michelle
3. A FREE audio: *Washing the Dishes to Wash the Dishes: An Exercise in Mindfulness*
4. *BONUS gift: get copies of the worksheets from the book*

Get the support and tools you need to get what you want

My research has shown that books all by themselves do not support women in getting what they want in life. That is why I've included 3 special gifts that no one else has access to so that you have the additional support necessary to get what you want.

Your Free Gift URL:
http://drmichellecleere.com/free-gifts/

Acknowledgements

So many people helped with the creation of this book. Many don't even know it.

I want to thank all of the people at Syracuse University Hospital who spent endless hours helping me get through severe anorexia. Thanks to all of the professors and colleagues during my time at Onondaga Community College, SUNY Cortland and John F. Kennedy University. A huge thank you to Jeff Le Roux for believing in me and helping me finish my PhD. You may never know how grateful I am for your kindness and generosity.

I would like to thank all of the colleagues and friends who have supported me throughout my life. Many have come and gone but many of you are still here after all these years. ☺ There are too many to list here and knowing me, I'd forget someone so I am not going to list them but you know who you are.

Lauren Carpenter initially helped me to figure out how to market and brand my business. She's is the creator of my fabulous website. Ana Rosenberg is my new creative marketing coach helping me maneuver through the next, new phase of my business.

In the production of this book there are several people who tirelessly spend hours helping me pull it together: Jen Sobel and Vivian Grimaldo helped me with content. Alicia Dunams helped me with all the nuts and bolts (Bestseller in a Weekend ROCKS!). My sister Lydia Puhak was gracious and brave enough to do all the editing. I am appreciative of her love and compassion for me and my work. Nancy Holliday designed the book cover and artwork. She is an amazing artist with amazing patience. Thanks Laurie Johnson for putting together the forward.

I am so thankful to my clients who took the time to provide the most amazing testimonials of our work together. I love my work and I love my clients. You are all freaking amazing people and I've been fortunate to spend time helping you become even more amazing.

Everything that has taken place in my life is the reason I am where I am today. Without all of it, I may not be here. Thank you!

6/26/14

Nancy
We've been a part of each other's
life for many years now. I am so
glad you are a constant, supportive,
loving person in my life.
There is no way this book would be
possible without. Thank you for all your
hard work. Love you Cleeve xo

12427198R00122

Made in the USA
San Bernardino, CA
17 June 2014